# CONNECTIONS

**Also by Faith Winters**

Abundance

Connections

Fundamentals

Keeping Calm

Restoration

Trauma Healing Series - Book 3

# CONNECTIONS

Master the Art of Relationship

**Faith Winters**

www.FaithfulHabits.com

Trauma Healing Series - Book 3

CONNECTIONS: Master the Art of Relationship

Author: Faith Winters

Copyright © 2021 Faith Winters

First Printing: August 2021

Paperback  ISBN: 978-1-7377164-4-0

Library of Congress Control Number:

Faithful Habits Press

www.faithfulhabits.com

*Editor: Rochelle Dean*

*Cover Art by Evelyn Drambarean*

Contact the author at: Author@faithfulhabits.com

To order bulk copies for groups contact: Info@faithfulhabits.com

# About the author

**Faith Winters** is a mental health professional with nearly two decades of experience. She is an expert who has taught thousands of people how to live calmer, more fulfilling lives. She is an author of books focused on helping people to heal and grow. Faith has mentored and trained many other mental health professionals.

## Why I wrote this Trauma Healing Book Series

I grew up in an abusive home. The childhood wounds to our hearts and self-worth rarely heal on their own. They need some intentional help to heal. As a child, I learned ways to cope with the wounds. While those coping mechanisms allowed me to survive as a child, those same learned habits crippled my life as an adult and made each day harder than it needed to be. The wounds of the past were not healed, just buried. To heal I needed to learn the fundamental principles of how to live a healthy life that removes barriers to growth. Through a healing process, I learned how to value myself, how to have boundaries with others and how to find the freedom of wise decision-making. Now I live a calm, happy life with a calling to help others to escape the pains of the past.

God has comforted me, and I want to help others be comforted as they heal and grow. I want there to be less suffering in the world. My journey has uniquely qualified me to help others move toward a healthier life.

- **Experience in living for decades with struggles** – I grew up in traumatic circumstances and spent decades as an adult dealing with anxiety, panic attacks, and PTSD (Post Traumatic Stress Disorder). In the midst of those painful years, I learned valuable lessons in surviving struggles and the need for healing.
- **Healing process** – I went through psychoeducational classes, extensive reading, and professional mental health therapy. As my anxiety ended, and the panic attacks ceased, and the PTSD was finally gone, I wanted to help others to escape the traumas of the past and to heal and grow.
- **Education** – I then decided to attend university to get a master's degree in counseling so I would have the professional therapeutic skills to help others heal from trauma in effective ways.
- **Experience in teaching these key skills to others** – For nearly two decades I have worked as a professional counselor and have taught thousands of people how to deal with struggles, heal from trauma and live calmer, healthier, happier lives even in the midst of struggles.

As you learn more about your rights as a human, your mind may experience a shift from being a victim of trauma toward the possibility of a happy and healthy life. All of the principles in this book will help to build strength within you as you grow and heal. It will take some effort on your part to live out your rights and responsibilities, but the principles to move forward are here in your hands. If you apply these principles, it may literally change the course of your life and have a positive effect on people around you.

# Trauma Healing Series Outline

This **Trauma Healing Series** explores the differences between a healthy, functional life and a wounded life impacted by the lingering effects of bullying, abuse, trauma, neglect, domestic violence, substance use, and chaos. The series is designed to help lower the barriers that hinder growth and healing so you can move forward toward the freedom of thriving.

*Trauma is any disturbing experience that results in significant fear, helplessness, dissociation, confusion, or other disruptive feelings intense enough to have a long-lasting negative effect on a person's attitudes, behavior, and other aspects of functioning. Traumatic events may challenge a person's view of the world as a reasonable, safe, and predictable place.*

Many individuals experience trauma during their lifetimes. Although some people exposed to trauma demonstrate few lingering symptoms, other people—especially those who have experienced repeated, chronic, or multiple traumas—are more likely to have many struggles and after-effects, including emotional distress, substance abuse, and physical and mental health problems.

Many individuals who seek help and recovery have histories of trauma. But they often do not recognize the impact their trauma has had on their lives. Either they do not draw connections between their past trauma and their current struggles, or they may try to avoid thinking about hard times altogether. Time alone does not heal most trauma; healthy processing is a part of the healing dynamic.

***Processing the past*** *is the act of making sense of an experience and putting it to rest, which includes achieving the resolution needed to move on from a traumatic experience. If some aspect of trauma is not processed, it may continue to cause problems in the present until it can be put to rest.*

## Books in the Trauma Healing Series

### Trauma Healing Series - Book 1

# FUNDAMENTALS

*Escape the Lingering Effects of Bullying, Abuse or Trauma*

By learning your fundamental human rights, developing inner awareness of your strengths, and understanding the contrast to past chaos you will step into a life with security, significance, and happiness. Explore how to have more peace within yourself, better relationships with others, and more freedom and contentment, no matter what is going on around you.

### Trauma Healing Series - Book 2

# RESTORATION

*Living as Designed, in Joy and Peace*

You are designed to have peace and joy and be able to heal from the wounds of life. Look deeply into your uniqueness. Put to rest the old wounds that hinder your healing  and trap you into painful patterns of responding to life. By exploring and adopting healthy patterns instead, you will live your best life after trauma. You will have restoration.

**Trauma Healing Series - Book 3**

## CONNECTIONS

*Master the Art of Relationship*

When you do what it takes to develop wholesome social habits and essential boundary skills, you can have good relationships at home, at work, and with friends, family, and that special someone, no matter what your past relationships were like. By learning key skills for a healthy lifestyle and safe, healthy relationships, you will unlock the power of community to discover your connected place in the world.

**Trauma Healing Series - Book 4**

## ABUNDANCE

*Create Confidence, Contentment and Happiness*

You can have the freedom of contentment, recognizing and enjoying the abundance of life around you. Contentment is not the fulfillment of what you want but the realization of what you already have. By using the principles of abundance in this book, you will derive riches that go far beyond the temporary rewards of success and create lasting happiness in any situation.

# Table of Contents

WHAT THIS BOOK IS ABOUT .............................. ix

YOUR RIGHTS AS A HUMAN BEING ................ xiii

**PART ONE : The Basic Skills of being Connected**

CHAPTER 1................................................................1

To Whom and How are we Connected

CHAPTER 2................................................................9

Integrity and Truth

CHAPTER 3..............................................................17

Respect Strengthens Connections

CHAPTER 4..............................................................23

Responsibility

CHAPTER 5..............................................................31

Love and Loyalty

CHAPTER 6..............................................................37

Core Values and Connections

**PART TWO : Social Community – Connecting Safely**

CHAPTER 7..............................................................45

We need other people

CHAPTER 8..............................................................53

Being a Safe Person

CHAPTER 9..............................................................61

Finding that Special Someone

CHAPTER 10............................................................67

Healthy, Committed Relationship

CHAPTER 11............................................................ 73
Children
CHAPTER 12............................................................ 79
Supporting Connections

**PART THREE : Connections Disrupted - Abuse and Safety**
CHAPTER 13............................................................ 91
Healthy Connections vs. Abusive Interactions
CHAPTER 14.......................................................... 101
Abuse, Manipulation, Guilt
CHAPTER 15.......................................................... 107
Why People Stay in Abusive Relationships
CHAPTER 16.......................................................... 113
What Does It Take to Get Out?
CHAPTER 17.......................................................... 119
Healing After Disruption
CHAPTER 18.......................................................... 125
Life After Healing
Afterword : Faith's Story of Connections.............. 131

*Let us make mankind in our image*

## WHAT THIS BOOK IS ABOUT

We are created to be connected. Our first existence is connection with our creator from inside our mother's womb. From there, we connect with mother and other important people in our lives. The lingering effects of past bullying, abuse, trauma, or trouble can damage our ability to connect in healthy ways. They can cause a lack of trust, a feeling of danger from connection. And yet we yearn to be connected. The word connections refers to how we interact with ourselves and with others. Theses connections can be beneficial or hindering; they can be safe, neutral, or unsafe.

Many people have experienced disrupted connections, and problems in their lives that create pain, and lingering emotional wounds. The wounded patterns of connecting behavior that follow can last for decades. These wounds are rarely healed by time alone.

Understanding how to connect to self and to others can lead to changing to a healthy pattern of behavior.

This book explores what it means to be connected: first with ourselves and then to others. We will also look at what happens to safety when connections are disrupted by abuse and trauma. *Connections* looks closely at what it takes to develop wholesome social habits and essential boundary skills. You can have good relationships no matter what your past relationships were like. Through this book, you will learn key skills for a healthy, connected lifestyle and safe, healthy relationships.

*Connections* was written to help people find the richness of a connected life that is available to all of us. Learning the skills of healthy ways of ways of connecting will bring joy and happiness. As the third book in the Trauma Healing Series, *Connections* will look in depth at the primary principles on which a healthy, connected life is based, the way we are designed to function. The other three books in the series: *Fundamentals, Restoration,* and *Abundance,* explore the foundational principles and go deeply into the skill-building process in healing old wounds and moving into a pattern of healthy living.

Abuse thrives in isolation and breaks the connections between people, even to connections within ourselves. The childhood wounds to our heart and self-worth do not often heal on their own. They need some intentional help to heal. As a child, I learned ways to cope with the wounds I'd received. While those were functional skills that allowed me to survive as a child, those same coping habits crippled my life as an adult and made each day harder than it needed to be. We need to learn how to live a healthy life that removes barriers to healing. Through a healing process, I learned how to value myself, how to have boundaries with others, and how to find the freedom of wise decision making. Now I live a calm, happy life, well-connected with others and with a calling to help others to escape the pains of the past.

The solution to a traumatic history is not "just forget the past." The solution is putting the past to rest so the old coping patterns of the past do not continue to hinder your present. You learn how to build and strengthen within yourself the resilience to face life's troubles with an unshakable confidence. We do that in connection to others who can support and comfort us.

*Praise be to the God and Father of our Lord Jesus Christ, the Father of compassion and the God of all comfort, who comforts us in all our troubles, so that we can comfort those in any trouble with the comfort we ourselves receive from God.*

*2 Corinthians 1:3,4*

# YOUR RIGHTS AS A HUMAN BEING

In the first book of this trauma healing series, *FUNDAMENTALS*, we explored in depth our basic rights as humans. In the second book , *RESTORATION*, we built on those foundational principles as we explored how we are designed to heal. Now in the third book CONNECTIONS we look at how these principles apply in our interactions with others.

**Individual rights** include how we interact with ourselves, the boundaries we set up and understanding what is our own and what is not ours. Individual rights include the basic ways we can expect to be treated and the basic ways we treat others, with dignity and respect.

- You have the right to be you and to love and be loved.
- You have the right to make mistakes, to be human – not perfect.
- You have the right to say NO.

- You have the right to choose your own values and beliefs.
- You have the right to your own feelings and opinions and to express them.
- You have the right to change your mind and your life.

**Relational rights** are the rights that we have as we relate to other people: family, friends, bosses, children, parents, neighbors, a significant other, and all the different people that we interact with in life. Relational rights provide healthy ways to interact with people.

- You have the right to be safe, to be treated with dignity and respect.
- You have the right to healthy friendships.
- You have the right to choose when and how your body is touched.
- You have the right to treat yourself as well as you treat others.
- You have the right not to be responsible for other adults' choices, feelings, and behavior.
- You have the right to feel angry and leave if you are treated abusively.

**Freedom rights** are the freedoms that we have individually and collectively to make our own choices of what we want to do and how we want to move forward in our life. These are the responsibilities and choices we have as adults.

- You have the right to your own privacy, personal space, and time.
- You have the right to make your own decisions about your life.

- You have the right to ask questions about anything that affects your life.
- You have the right to request what you want.
- You have the right to earn and control your own resources.
- You have the right to not be liked by everyone.

*Connections*
*How we interact with*
*ourselves and with others.*
*Theses connections can be*
*beneficial or hindering,*
*safe, neutral, or unsafe.*

# PART ONE

## The Basic Skills of being Connected

We begin our study of Connections looking at what kinds of connections we have and who we are connected to. We will explore individual behaviors and the general skill set that affect how we connect in healthy ways.

# CHAPTER 1

---

## To Whom and How are we Connected

We are connected to many people in many different ways. It is good to take a look at each of these connections and how they are interacting in our lives.

### Many layers of connection

The basic relationships skills in healthy connections begin with respect for ourselves and others. The levels of closeness and vulnerability is different with the different layers of relationship connections we all have in life. But the attitude of healthy relationships and the essential boundary setting within relationships is similar.

Some relationship skills are general and apply to all of our connections. Other skills apply only to specific connections. One thing all these connections have in common is that we affect others by the way we interact with them, and they affect us by the way they interact with us.

Lets begin here with an overview of the many people we have connections with. This list will vary from person to person, but this will give a general idea of who we need to consider.

## Who We Have Connections With

Family connections – biological, legal, and chosen

- Extended family connections
- Dependents – children or vulnerable adults

Significant other connection

- Committed relationship

Friend connections

- Close friends
- Casual friends
- Friendly acquaintances

Work, job, career connections

- Co-workers and colleagues
- Customers
- Vendors

Business connections

- Professional Services – medical, legal etc.
- Services and trade
- Gig workers

Community connections

- People in our community
- Other drivers, people we walk by
- Other shoppers at stores
- Neighbors

Governmental connections

- Local – Neighborhood, City, County
- Regional – State
- National – Federal

## How We Are Connected

Our attitude toward other people greatly affects our all relationships: our significant other, family, the clerk in a store we see occasionally, down to governmental people we only interact with rarely. Our attitude and our choice of how we behave toward others in general will greatly affect our own happiness and sense of feeling at peace with our place in the world. Consider these words.

*Jesus replied: "'Love the Lord your God with all your heart and with all your soul and with all your mind.' This is the first and greatest commandment. And the second is like it: 'Love your neighbor as yourself.' All the Law and the Prophets hang on these two commandments."*

*Matthew 22:37-40*

When we have an attitude of love, of respect, and of considering others as valuable as ourselves, our relationships tend to go well. Think about what Jesus said: "Love your neighbor as yourself." As talked about in the second book of this Trauma Healing series, *Restoration,* this command is not to love others instead of ourselves. It is loving others *as* ourselves. While our very first connection is with God—he loves us, and we love him—our second is to love each other as ourselves.

Loving ourselves is not about just doing what I want when I want, or being selfish, greedy, or lazy. The healthy connection with ourselves is to love and respect ourselves and out of that to show that same love and respect to others.

In Mark 10:29-37, in the story of the good Samaritan, Jesus showed us that loving our neighbor is being concerned about other people, helping them, and seeking the best for them in their time of need. Therefore, what matters is not just "feeling" love—it is also "doing" love. Love is not just how I make myself feel positive loving feelings, but rather how I take loving actions. I do not even have to feel loving in order to treat others with compassion and respect. That is a choice of will, a decision I make. However, my feeling may soon follow my decisions. I like how that is expressed in this passage.

*Dear children, let us not love with words or speech but with actions and in truth.*

*1 John 3:18*

When we take action to tret each other well we are living out our respect for ourselves and for others.

We all desire to love and be loved. An attitude of love is the sound foundation for all our connections. When someone loves us, they will not ask us to do things that are against our best interest. They will not support us in doing things that are wrong. Someone who loves us is kind and gentle to us; they support and nurture us in all the things that are right. The following is a beautiful description of the attributes of love.

*Love is patient, love is kind. It does not envy, it does not boast, it is not proud. It does not dishonor others, it is not self-seeking, it is not easily angered, it keeps no record of wrongs. Love does not delight in evil but rejoices with the truth. It always protects, always trusts, always hopes, always perseveres.*

*1 Corinthians 13:4-7*

Learning to love is a more than an attitude of heart it is a choice of will and a skill set that we learn and develop each day when we make intentional choices to be kind, gentle  and loving in our connections.

## Respecting Others and Setting Boundaries

Boundaries in our life define what is mine and not mine, what we are responsible for and what we are not responsible for. Good boundaries define how much we let other people have access to in our lives. When we have healthy boundaries, we can risk getting close to people and letting people get close to us.

When we have experienced betrayal, abuse, bullying, or trauma as a child, we may never have been allowed to develop boundaries or had our boundaries respected. While we yearn for connection with people, we know that people can hurt us. The world can feel unsafe. We may bounce back and forth between trusting people too much, and getting hurt again, to trusting no one and being isolated and alone. There is another choice. We can connect safely with healthy boundaries.

Out on range land grazed a bull. He looked the size of a big car. Bulls can be aggressive and territorial, so we could not get close to him, look into his eyes, or see his muscles up close. In a fenced area at the state fair was another bull. He, too, was huge. But this bull we could get close enough to look in his eyes, see the strength of his muscles, and hear the sounds of his breathing. Why was it safe to get closer to the bull at the fair? Because there was a strong boundary between him and us. That fence, that boundary, allowed us to get close and still be safe.

Setting healthy boundaries is what allows us to develop healthy relationships with people. We can set up how close we will let people get to us in our lives. We let them in a little way and see how they behave. Those who are respectful we may let in closer.

This information was explored more in depth in the Trauma Healing Series book one, *Fundamentals* and book two, *Restoration*.

**In summary**

Here's what we already learned about connecting with people. The rest of this book will deepen this knowledge. We are connected to many different people, in many different layers of connection. The calm, respectful, loving attitude of healthy relationships sets a tone for our interactions, and good boundaries are essential within relationships. We get to choose how closely we want to be connected with different people. Having good boundaries is an important skill that allows us to connect safely.

# CHAPTER 2

---

## Integrity and Truth

One of the essential skills in relationships is honesty. Having integrity and truth allows us to build trust and make healthy connections. Dishonesty, deceit, lying, and manipulation erode trust and destroy connections.

### Integrity in Connections

In all our connections, integrity is a vital characteristic. Integrity allows people to trust us and allows us to trust other people. Healthy people have a level of integrity that makes making healthy connections a normal part of their life.

To have integrity means three things:

1) **Integrity means to be honest and upright**, someone you can trust. When you have

integrity, people can rely on you. You are consistently responsible.

2) **Integrity also means to be integrated.** All of who you are is integrated in all your life. Who you are on Sunday morning at church is the same as who you are at a Friday-night party.

3) **Integrity also means to be whole and fit for our purpose.** We say that a water bottle has integrity when it does not leak. It is whole and fit for its purpose.

## Integrity is a learned skill

Integrity is important for making good connections, and integrity is a learned skill. To have integrity is to stand out from the crowd and keep your values, no matter what the world around you is doing. In a healthy, nurturing home, children see parents with integrity. They see it modeled; they are taught the specific skills of integrity and they grow up with integrity. However, not everybody had the luxury of growing up in a healthy nurturing home. Also the examples in entertainment media and often in politics may fail to show the modeling of integrity. No matter their history or examples, though, anyone can learn the skills of integrity.

## Honest and Upright

Someone who is honest, and upright is a trustworthy person who can be relied on to be consistently responsible. That is a learned skill. You start by being faithful in small things. You learn at first in little things and then you can apply that skill in bigger things.

- **True to your word.** Having integrity is to do what you said you would do. But understand something about wisdom and integrity; Integrity is to do what you promised, no matter the cost to yourself. Wisdom is learning not to make promises.
- **Showing up** when you said you would and being ready to do what is needed when you get there, whether at work or at home. A person with integrity is someone who can be relied on.
- **Not taking what is not yours.** We hear the phrase: 'finders keepers losers weepers,' but that does not show integrity. It is not honest and upright. When you find something, the one thing you do know about it is this: it is not yours. Someone else has lost it. To have integrity is to try to find the owner, or turn it into the lost and found authorities.
- **Doing the right thing** even when no one is looking. Having integrity is being aware of what is right, in line with truth and honesty and doing that whether anyone else would ever know or not.
- **Respecting privacy.** For example: If you are at somebody's house and you see their diary sitting open, out on the table and there is nobody around for a few minutes, respectful integrity is respecting their privacy enough to not even look at it. Again, it is not yours.
- **Not coveting or stealing.** Somebody who can be trusted does not entertain thoughts of wanting

what somebody else has. When you covet someone else's stuff, that is only a few steps away from trying to deceive, cheat, steal and take their stuff. To have integrity is to recognize that it is their stuff and to not want somebody else's stuff.

## To be Integrated

Another part of integrity is to be integrated. It means that I behave the same way around my friends as I do around strangers. I behave the same way with business connections as with personal connections. Some people say, "Nothing personal, it is just business." They use that attitude as an excuse to behave badly and to cheat. Having integrity integrated throughout our lives means we are just as honest and kind with strangers, or in business as we are at home and with our friends.

Being integrated means that the vocabulary, attitude, compassion, and respectfulness that I use day in and day out at work is the same vocabulary, attitude, compassion, and respectfulness I use Sunday morning in church, and the same vocabulary, attitude, compassion, and respectfulness I use while partying Friday night with friends.

## Whole and Complete, Fit for our Purpose

Another part of integrity is about being whole and complete and fit for our purpose. We get to choose to grow toward wholeness and a life of purpose. To be whole and fit for our purpose is about finding the wounds that hinder us, acknowledging them, and working to let God heal them. It is also about learning and growing. Anything that is alive grows and changes. We are created to be alive, grow, learn and change as we move toward wholeness and being fit for a purpose. What is your purpose in life?

My purpose is to know, love and follow Jesus. Within that purpose I work towards my mission helping there to be less suffering in the world. To be more fit for my purpose, I went through a process of healing, working with a therapist. Then I went to school to get further education, and worked under supervision to increase my therapeutic skills.

All of these skills of integrity are ongoing, intentional choices. The world around us will constantly provide opportunities for you to damage your integrity. You get to decide whether to allow that damage. What would it take for you to sell your integrity? We get invited to sell our integrity all the time. The offer is in the world around us everywhere. If you are going to have integrity, you will have to work at keeping it strong all the time. It is a choice of will and a skill that we strengthen by constant use

## Wisdom and Integrity

Integrity is about learning to do what you promised you were going to do, no matter the cost to yourself. When it comes to promises, wisdom may mean, not promising. Wisdom remembers not to promise something when you may not be able to follow through. Having integrity means people can rely on what you say you will do. That also means they can rely on you to say 'No' if you are not going to be able to follow through.

## Behavior that Damages Connections

Dishonesty, deceit, lying, cheating, and stealing damage our healthy connections with people. When the truth is manipulated or twisted in order to get a specific result, connections are damaged in the process because trust has been broken. In all of our healthy connections, trust, honesty, and integrity are vital.

Sometimes people will say, 'I do not lie.' while they argue about the exact words they said and try to justify deceit. But integrity is not about the exact words used, it is about the intent to be honest or the intent to deceive.

If I tell you that I was traveling at well over a hundred miles an hour along the freeway. Every word of that is true. You may have a certain image in your mind of reckless speed. But if I do not mention I was a passenger in a small airplane at 500 feet altitude, you really do not have the truth. That is a different image of the necessary speed of the travel.

Honesty is about giving an accurate information about what you are talking about. Not trying the distort the truth and give a different impression.

## The Effect of Mistakes on Integrity and Connections

Everyone makes mistakes. Honest mistakes are a normal part of life. When we try to pass off dishonesty as an honest mistake, it damages trust. When we try to sneak, lie, and hide our own mistakes, it damages trust. When we try to pass our own mistakes off and blame someone else for them, it damages trust doubly.

Some people have had their trust broken so often it may be hard for them to accept any mistake as an honest mistake. That can make it more difficult for us to work to repair a mistake.

The healthy way to deal with your mistakes is to own that you made a mistake. Ask what you can do to repair the mistake. Be willing to deal with the consequences of your mistake. In this way you have the best chance of keeping a healthy connection while preserving your own integrity. It can feel hard to admit you made a mistake when you fear you will get in trouble. But the instant you made the mistake, you were already in trouble. Here we are discussing the best way out of the trouble you are already in. Denying the mistake or hiding, lying, or deceiving is just adding more trouble to the situation.

Giving grace to people who make mistakes

Everyone makes mistakes. How would you like people to treat you when you make a mistake? Grace is unmerited favor, which means treating someone kindly when they have not done anything to deserve it. Giving grace to other people who make mistakes makes connections healthier. Helping them to work through the process of correcting the mistake in a kind, patient, and respectful attitude will strengthen your connection.

> *Above all, love each other deeply, because*
> *love covers over a multitude of sins.*
> *1 Peter 4:8*

## In summary

One of the essential skills in healthy relationship connections is honesty. Having integrity and truth allows us to build trust, make, and strengthen healthy connections. Dishonesty, deceit, lying, and manipulation erode the trust and destroy connections.

# CHAPTER 3

---

## Respect Strengthens Connections

All people want to be treated with respect. Respect strengthens connections. Respect is a way of treating or thinking about someone with regard for the fact that they have as much value as you have. Respect is polite behavior, treating people in a positive manner that acknowledges them for who they are, and giving due regard for their feelings, wishes, rights, or traditions.

### Respect Is Earned

Respect must be earned. That statement is only half true. Respect is both given and earned. We give respect first. Respect is a choice and a lifestyle. The level of respect that we treat others with says more about us than them. When we treat ourselves with respect, we make it easier for others to treat us with respect.

When I meet someone for the first time, I treat them with the average level of respect I have decided to treat all people in the world with. This basic level says something about my own character choices, nothing else. As I get to know the person better, my level of respect for them may increase or decrease dependent upon how they behave, what I learn about them and how they treat me.

But the maximum level of that decrease is again dependent upon my own character, not theirs. I have a minimum standard of respect that I treat all people out of reverence for their creator. Even if my respect for a person has fallen to my minimal level, I recognize their value as a human being and I will be civil, polite, and kind. I may not have much regard for their skills in a particular area; I may not like their behavior or opinion; I may choose to be more formal, distant, and reserved; I may set up protective boundaries; and I may choose not to be in their company any more than necessary. But I still recognize their basic value as a human. I recognize that our core value is the same before God.

In the same way, the maximum level my respect increases is also dependent on how I see all people as the same before their creator. No one is worth more and no one is worth less than any other person. Their basic value is all the same as mine. I may increase my respect for their skills, for their character, or for their compassion. I may seek to recognize and honor those things in their life and use their example as something for me to aspire to and want to grow more like them. But our core value is the same before God.

## Cultural Diversity and Respect

Respect has different expression in different cultures. In my home, I want to show respect and hospitality by showing a guest to the best chair in my house. That chair is a recliner which I encourage friends to sit back put your feet up and feel at home, and I will put my feet up too. I am showing my hospitality by this casual and friendly way. However, in some parts of the world, it is considered rude to show the sole of your foot to others. If someone from that part of the world comes to my house and I use a footstool and put my feet up, they may feel disrespected. I am trying to send a respectful message of hospitality within my culture, but my guest would be receiving a message of disrespect filtered through their culture.

In order to make healthy connections with people, it helps to understand a bit about the culture of the people you regularly interact with. This includes talking with them about culture, learning more so they will be able to experience the level of respect I want to show.

## Respect for Property

The connections we have with others is affected by the way we treat property—our own and property that belongs to others. Our connections to our community are affected negatively when we treat public property disrespectfully. When we damage or mistreat someone else's property, we are damaging our connection with those people as well. Public property belongs to all of us. It is not okay for any one of us to damage or treat it disrespectfully. If every one of us damaged public property even a little, soon all public property would be trashed. It is there for all of us to use respectfully.

## Respect for the Place You Live

If you rent a place to live, what does it mean to treat it respectfully? When we rent a place to live we are agreeing to take a basic level of care of the place as a place to live. That includes keeping it clean and not damaging it. It is a demonstration of your own integrity, your own respect, the level of care that you take of a home. A responsible person will be careful to not damage property.

At the end of your time there, you should return it clean and in the condition in which you received it. It is generally a responsible practice to do a walk through with the landlord just before you move in, noting the condition of the home and a walk through after you have moved out showing the condition you are leaving the place. That builds connections with landlords and can help you to have good references. Just as tenants have a responsibility to respect a dwelling, it is a landlord's responsibility to provide a place fit to live in. This walkthrough shows respect to both parties.

Having respect for your agreements builds connections. When you agree to rent a dwelling, you pay the rent on or before it is due each month. When you order utilities, you agree to pay for them in a timely manner. Paying your utility bills on time (or a few days ahead) builds your reputation with service providers and can affect the amount of any deposits you are required to provide.

## Respect is not Context Dependent

Respect is dependent on your internal values not on what is going on around you at the moment. Respect is about how you treat other people, even when things are not going to your liking, even when you are tired, frustrated, and feeling upset. When the person you are speaking with is not helping you resolve your problem, you must be extra careful to continue to treat people with respect. It can be tempting to take your frustration out on people who are not being helpful with unkind words and an aggressive attitude, but that will not help you get your needs met. Handling it with grace in a civil and polite way will make that other person's day a little easier, and it may help you have a better chance to get what you need.

## In Summary

Respect is a way of treating or thinking about someone with regard for the fact that they have as much value as you have. Respect is polite behavior, treating people in a positive manner that acknowledges them for who they are, giving due regard for their feelings, wishes, rights, or traditions. All people want to be treated with respect. Respect strengthens connections.

# CHAPTER 4

## Responsibility

Responsibility deeply affects our ability to have good connections with others. We are responsible for anything we have choice over. Responsibility is having a duty to deal with or have control over, or being the person who is answerable or accountable for something within your control, power, or management. It is the ability or opportunity make decisions without authorization and to act independently.

Being responsible means that people can count on you being where you said you would be, when you said you would be there. Other people never have to wonder or worry about where you are and what you are doing. Responsible people choose to be accountable for their own actions. Responsible people take care of their own tasks and help out other people. Therefore they are trusted and looked up to.

## Lack of Responsibility

A lack of responsibility affects our connections in many ways. Other people may feel like they need to protect themselves around you, because you are not trustworthy. They cannot rely on the things you say and therefore do not pay much attention to you when you talk. A relationship with someone irresponsible is often shallow and fragile. The relationships tend to stay guarded and are easily broken. We do not invite untrustworthy people very deeply into our lives. Therefore, being responsible strengthens relationship connections because trust lets us risk getting close to people. They can rely on us, and we can rely on them.

## Responsible to God

God has entrusted us with free will and we get to choose the way we will go. He entrusts parents with children to raise and care for. He entrusts us with the ability to be creative and to work. Therefore we are responsible to God for the choices we make.

## Responsible to Ruling Authorities

The core laws of any nation are generally for the benefit of the people. They establish how people can live together. Each resident is responsible for their behavior and how it affects their community and nation.

## Responsible Use of Time

Responsible use of time is about being able to do the things you need to do at the times they need to be done. For instance, it is important to organize your time so you meet friends and family when you said you would be there, not making people wait for you. It builds connections where people can rely on when you said you would be somewhere. That is respectful and courteous of their time.

Responsible management of time is more than a courtesy, though: it is a tool that responsible people use for the benefit of themselves and others. A successful worker described his time management at work as: Arriving on a job site early enough to put your personal items away, look over your day's tasks, check in with site supervisor, and go to your workstation to make sure it is ready for your day at least 5 minutes before you expect to start work. You should be ready for your work, getting yourself calm and centered, ready to focus on your task. Therefore, your boss and co-workers experience you as a consistent, competent worker they can depend on.

He does not rush in at the last minute, searching for things he needs, becoming just another piece of chaos in workplace. Coming in at the last minute or being late lowers trust and connection. It can affect co-workers and inconvenience others. Think about how the things you do affect others in your workplace. Do you affect them for good or for ill?

## Responsible to Work

*In the name of the Lord Jesus Christ, we command you, brothers and sisters, to keep away from every believer who is idle and disruptive and does not live according to the teaching you received from us. For you yourselves know how you ought to follow our example. We were not idle when we were with you, nor did we eat anyone's food without paying for it. On the contrary, we worked night and day, laboring and toiling so that we would not be a burden to any of you. We did this, not because we do not have the right to such help, but in order to offer ourselves as a model for you to imitate. For even when we were with you, we gave you this rule: "The one who is unwilling to work shall not eat." We hear that some among you are idle and disruptive. They are not busy; they are busybodies. Such people we command and urge in the Lord Jesus Christ to settle down and earn the food they eat. And as for you, brothers and sisters, never tire of doing what is good.*

*2 Thessalonians 3:6-13*

When we work responsibly there is a sense of fulfilment that strengthens inside of us. Our place in the world feels more at peace and we respect ourselves more. Working is an important component of being human.

There are times and situations which make may make earning our own living difficult;

- Injuries, illness, physical or mental disabilities for example.
- Losing your job

- Not being able to find a job
- Being in a recovery community
- Being a parent with small children

But in all of these situations we still have the choice of our attitude toward what we can contribute to make our own life better. We can still be responsible to do what we are capable of doing. There is usually a certain level of work we are capable of even without a job, or perhaps even if disabled or in recovery. It is about doing as much as you can for yourself and those entrusted to your care, so you are not an unnecessary burden on others.

Even if we cannot do anything we can have a responsible and grateful attitude toward those who help us in ways we are unable to help ourselves. When we are thoughtful and grateful it keeps us away from being idle and being busybodies.

## Responsible with Money

Healthy, responsible money handling skills are important to connections. The basic money skills of earning your own living, caring for your responsibilities, caring for those who depend on you, and having enough for your needs are vital. Once you get the most basic of needs met, it is not about how much money is brought into the family. After that, it is about not spending more than the amount that comes in, being able to care for needs, and having some money set aside for generosity and savings. Only then does a responsible money-handler look at what might be available for discretion spending on things that are wanted.

Responsible money handling is about knowing where the resources are coming from and where they are going, keeping records so you know that information. Responsible people pay their bills on time – meaning that the rent gets to the landlord a couple of days before it is due. The utility bills are paid a couple of days before the due date, vehicle insurance is paid regularly, and money is set aside for the groceries needed each week. Responsible money handling also sets aside a small amount each payday to build up an emergency fund.

## Responsible Family Income Handling

In healthy families, the adults provide for the needs of the family. Income and resources are spent in a way that benefits the needs of the family, not just one person. Take the example of a husband and wife with three very young children. One adult may work outside the home while the other one stays at home and cares for their children. The one income is spent on the needs of the family. It is not thought of as "my income" or "your income." It is thought of as "our income." They look at the family's expenses together. Resources are sorted out by needs as determined by both adults.

The adult who stays home is valued as equal to the one who brings in cash. They know that if the family had to pay out money for child care, it would take most of the wages the second adult would bring in. But the main value is that the children are being nurtured by a loving parent, not by a paid worker. The quality of the children's lives is greatly benefited by the effort *both* parents are putting into the family. These attitudes strengthen connections.

In a dysfunctional family with the same structure, where one person works outside the home for money and the other takes care of the children, the outside worker acts like they are the only one bringing in resources to the family and constantly gripes about any money spent on other family members' needs. The outside worker spends money on their own wants without regard for the family's needs and comfort. They may even spend the rent money on their own selfish pleasures, creating housing instability for the family. The adult taking care of the children can feel worthless since worth is being measured only by the cash brought in. These attitudes damage connections.

## In Summary

We are responsible for anything we have choice over. Being responsible means that people can count on you being where you said you would be, doing what you said you would do. Other people never have to wonder or worry about where you are and what you are doing. Responsible people can build deep and strong connections with other people. We are responsible to God for what he has entrusted us with. We are responsible to the ruling authorities of our nation. Responsible management of time is a tool for the benefit of ourselves and others. Being responsible with our work and money is important to healthy connections.

# CHAPTER 5

---

## Love and Loyalty

We all desire to love and be loved. Love is the strongest of connections. Love is more than just a sexual feeling. Love is not just 'me' focused, it is 'us' focused. When we love deeply, we want what is best for the other and we are loyal to them.

### Being in Love

When you love someone, you want to spend time with them, and you want them to spend time with the other important people in your life. You want them to be connected to your connections and you want to be connected to their connections. Loving someone means you want them to have what they need. One of their needs is to have good relationships with the other important people in their lives, so, you make it easy for them to see their friends and family. You make the effort to get along and be friends with their friends and their people.

You attitude changes from an "I" focus to a "we" focus. When people are in love, their lives are intertwined and the "we" becomes more a part of their life. One person described it as "He is more interested in me than he is in himself, and he is more interested in 'us' than he is in me." Each person in a relationship works to make the relationship work. Great relationships do not just happen on their own; it takes effort from each person. You may have heard that marriage is a 50/50 relationship. I suggest that is a wrong focus. Marriage is a 100/100 relationship. Both people put in the effort to nurture and support each other and the relationship.

When you love someone, you influence each other. You want to do what the other one does. You go to each other for support and help. You share the joys of your life, good news, bad news. You consider the other person before making decisions; you discuss important plans and come to decisions together. Being in love, you share deeply about your hopes, dreams, fears, past, and future. You want to share to the core of yourself with this wonderful other person and you want to know about them and be known beyond the surface.

It is good here to examine what it means to love. In English, love is a great interest and pleasure in something. We use that one word—love—to mean different concepts. We use it to say, "I love my child," and "I love the color green," and "I love to have a delicious sandwich for lunch." One word, but these are all different kinds of love. In the Greek of the Bible, there are a number of words to express different kinds of love.

Here are four Greek words that describe types of love:

- Eros – romantic, passionate love, from which we get our English word "erotic." Attraction based on sexual desire, affection, and tenderness felt by lovers.
- Storge – familial love, referring to natural or instinctual affection, such as the love of a parent toward offspring and children toward parents and siblings.
- Philia – the affectionate bond of friends, from which we get the name of the city "Philadelphia," the "city of brotherly love." It is about commitment, the love that binds one to another in enduring friendship, and strong affection for another.
- Agape – unconditional, self-sacrificing love that seeks only the welfare of the other. Unselfish loyal and benevolent concern for the good of another, to do what is in the long-term best interest of another. Not just a feeling, but a choice of will.

A healthy marriage has all of these kinds of love. Within a marriage and within a family, people will give up what they want at times in order to help another with what they need.

## Loyalty in Connections

Loyalty is important in a relationship. Loyalty shows up in a lot of different ways. One of the ways that loyalty shows up is when you are with your friends, you do not make fun of your spouse. You defend them in all that is right. You support and encourage them; you don't bring them up to shame or ridicule. You do not make jokes at their expense. In other words, their heart can safely trust in you.

Being loyal is also about being loyal to the values that you share. If your shared values include serving God, loving God, and following Jesus, then loyalty is about loyalty to the truth. Loyalty to God is more important than loyalty to the person. If the person that you love is doing something wrong, confronting them on that is a loving act.

Loyalty is about sharing and being together in all the things that are right. If you join someone in doing things that are wrong, they are damaging their own character and you are helping them to damage their character while damaging your own. This is a downward spiral for you both. Being loyal to doing what is right first will strengthen and build your relationship over the long term. Remember, love and loyalty are not always doing what they want in the moment, but instead doing what's in their long-term best interest.

### Selfishness or Sacrifice

Selfishness is lacking consideration for others; concerned chiefly with one's own personal profit or pleasure, devoted to or caring only for oneself; regardless of others, having a total disregard for anyone but yourself and not caring about anyone else's feelings. In relationships selfishness shows up in the way time and resources are handled, shared or not shared. Selfishness puts distance between people and lowers trust.

Sacrifice on the other hand, is a part of all good relationships. It's important to be aware of others' needs and willing to set aside your own wants and needs at times so you can do what is needed for them. In healthy relationships people are aware of how their behavior affects others and they are intentionally considerate of others.

## When the Garbage Needs to be Taken Out

When we discuss love, we talk of feelings, thinking of others, and wonderful things like that. But a good relationship also has simpler ways to show love and affection. Love includes the daily little kindnesses of taking out the garbage, cleaning up after ourselves, not leaving messes for others to deal with, sharing control, and sharing choices. When we give way to another person's preferences in the little things, that may make it easier for them to give way to your choices in the things you value more. Regular give and take is a part of a healthy relationship.

## Generosity in Relationships

Loving someone is also encouraging them in the way that they should go, helping to build them up, and equipping them. Maybe that means generously supporting someone with time and resources when they decide they need to go to school and get more education. Maybe that means encouraging someone as they're learning new skills or getting involved in a hobby you don't share. It's not trying to keep them with you all the time, but making space for them to breathe and to enjoy the things that they enjoy, even things they enjoy without you.

## Loving Enough to Confront

Another part of love is caring enough to confront someone when they're doing something that is damaging relationship. Confronting is speaking the truth in love, being able to talk it through, saying what's happening and how that's affecting the relationship, and being able to hear when they are saying to you when what you're doing might be damage the relationship. It is important to be able to talk through that, knowing that both of you are working toward having a healthy relationship. The skills of being able to have difficult, awkward, and messy conversations are an important part of connecting with others.

*Do not let any unwholesome talk come out of your mouths, but only what is helpful for building others up according to their needs, that it may benefit those who listen.*
*Ephesians 4:29*

## In Summary

We all desire to love and be loved. Love is the strongest of connections. Love is not just "me" focused; it is "us" focused. When we love deeply, we want what is best for the other and we are loyal to them. We love them enough to confront them when they are in error, and we love enough to always protect and support them in whatever is right.

# CHAPTER 6

## Core Values and Connections

In life, we make thousands of small decisions—right and wrong, beneficial or harmful, forward or back—that train our decision-making process. It is in these daily little decisions that we live out our values. We decide what process is important and what our objectives are. Then, when we find ourselves tired, sick, not thinking straight, and in crisis, these patterns of decision making influence our behavior to a high degree.

When we take the time to be intentional about the little decisions we make, it gives us the freedom to trust that our decision-making habits will align with our core values. Those core values can inform our decisions about the connections we make with other people

Values are what we have determined are important to us, the principles that help us decide what is useful, desirable, good or bad, right or wrong. Values have a major influence on a person's behaviors and attitudes and serve as broad guidelines in choosing what actions are best to do or what way is best to live. Therefore, our values affect the choices we make in which people to connect to and which people to limit connection with.

Aspirational values are the values we say we hold to, the ones we say are important to us. Behavioral values are the ones demonstrated by the things we do and the choices we make. It seems worthwhile to define the difference between an objective and a current activity. Objective is the overall goal in life. Current activity is what you are doing at any given time or day. In the best of worlds, our current activity is leading us toward our objective.

Here is a list of some common values, all of which can be aspirational or behavioral:

Individual Values

- Accuracy : To be correct in my opinions and beliefs
- Comfort : To have a pleasant and comfortable life
- Attractiveness : To be physically attractive
- Courage : To be brave and strong in the face of adversity
- Courtesy : To be considerate and polite toward others 21
- Creativity : To create new things or ideas

- Curiosity : To seek out, experience, and learn new things
- Dedication : The act of binding yourself to a course of action
- Diligence : Thorough and conscientious in whatever you do.
- Health : To be physically well and healthy
- Honesty : A high regard for truth, straightforwardness, sincerity,
- Hope : To maintain a positive and optimistic outlook
- Humility : To be modest and unassuming
- Integrity : Sound moral principle; uprightness, honesty, sincerity
- Patience : The capacity for enduring hardship or inconvenience

Connection Values
- Compassionate : Understanding and caring about suffering of others
- Commitment : To make enduring, meaningful commitments
- Accountability : Being responsible to answer for one's own actions
- Faithfulness : To be loyal and true in relationships
- Forgiveness : To be forgiving of others, not hold a grudge

- Friendship : To have close, supportive friends
- Trustworthy : Dependability, deserving of confidence
- Faith : A strong belief in a supernatural power
- Respect : Consideration, regard for other's rights, values, beliefs.
- Generosity : To give what I have to others
- Dependability : To be reliable and trustworthy
- God's Will : To seek and obey the will of God
- Helpfulness : Sense of concern for and outreach to the needs of others
- Loyalty : Faithfulness to another person or group
- Justice : Fairness, balance, equality treatment for all

Freedom Values

- Adventure : To have new and exciting experiences
- Humor : Ability to laugh at oneself and find humor in all things
- Fun : To play and have fun
- Autonomy : To be self-determined and independent
- Independence : Freedom from control or influence of others, self sufficient
- Advancement : Personal and professional growth

- Freedom : The power to act, speak or think as I want
- Knowledge : Learning new information and insights, and to contribute
- Leisure : To take time to relax and enjoy
- Recognition : To receive special attention, to feel important
- Growth : To keep changing and growing
- Change : To have a life full of change and variety
- Security : Having the essentials you need to live and be safe
- Success : Achieving your goals, position, favor, or eminence
- Wealth : Desire for substantial monetary income

## Values and Companions

*Do two walk together*
*unless they have agreed to do so?*
*Amos 3:3*

We will become like the people we spend a lot of time around, the ones we choose to have as our friends. If we are choosing people that share our core values, they will help us to strengthen and move toward our objectives in our lives, our goals, and becoming the human being that we want to be. If we choose to spend a lot of time around people who do not share our values, we are likely to become more like them, too. We find our values start to erode. We may think, well, this is just this little bit. It will not matter. We keep shifting a little bit at a time away from our core values, and pretty soon we find that we have shifted our core values completely to align with our new direction. This works either direction, for good or for ill.

*Do not be misled: "Bad company*
*corrupts good character."*
*1 Corinthians 15:33*

## In Summary

Knowing what our core values are and how they affect the connections that we make will either strengthen the connections that we have, or they will drag them apart. It helps to note who we choose who to spend a lot of time with. Are they helping me moving toward my objective in life or do they move me away from my objective?

# PART TWO

## Social Community – Connecting Safely

Now that we've looked at individual behaviors that affect how we connect, we will focus on our need for other people and how we connect to social community in healthy ways.

# CHAPTER 7

---

## We need other people

When we are alone, we can grow inward and become blind to the needs of others. It is easier to be selfish. We may become stuck in immaturity and our sense of morality may be adrift. Addictions can thrive in aloneness. Living is isolation can lead to despair, and to a life of quiet desperation. It is not good to be alone. We all need to be connected. We are designed to be connected to God and to other people. We need other people in our lives, more than just a significant other.

*As iron sharpens iron,*
*so one person sharpens another.*
*Proverbs 27:17*

When we are connected to others, they help us to thrive and see a wider context of life. Being connected, we heal, we grow, we can feel a sense of belonging and purpose. We have more opportunity for happiness. We see the needs and strengths of others and they see our needs and strengths. As we care for them, and they care for us, we become more kind, more loving, and more respectful. People with safe, healthy behaviors encourage and support us. They help us to stay centered, grow, and heal. We grow lopsided alone. We need to be around others, bumping into them enough to smooth off our lopsided areas so we are healthier.

However, not all people have learned or chosen safe behaviors. Not all people are good for us to be around. Bad companions corrupt good character. We tend to grow similar to those we spend the most time around. Are the people you spend time with helping you to move toward doing what is right, doing the next right thing, or are they leading you on a way that slides into wrong behaviors? Remember, we choose our companions and where the boundaries are with them.

The people we call friends are an important part of healthy connections.

There are many levels of friendship.

- **Everyone starts as a stranger**. When it comes to strangers, the boundaries are real far out, and they are really strong. We can be very polite and very civil if we need to talk to them, but the boundary is up strong because these people are not allowed access to my life.
- **Familiar faces**. These are people we do not know, but we recognize that we see them regularly: perhaps the person who walks their dog in our neighborhood, or the person at the bus stop each weekday. We do not know them.

They do not know us. But they seem to belong in our world. Familiar faces are not people we let into our life at all. They are in the peripheral; we see them out there. They seem like people we have seen before, so they seem to belong somewhere in our world, but the boundaries are far out here. Because we do not know these people, we do not allow them access to us closely. As we are around them more they may become friendly acquaintances.

- **Friendly acquaintances.** These include the worker at the grocery store we have been going to for ten years, or the librarian where we borrow books, people we greet casually Sunday morning as we walk by, etc. These are people we are around on a regular basis, but we do not really know them, and they do not really know us. We do not share any important information with friendly acquaintances. We chat about neutral shared experiences. We chat about the stuff we are around and doing in that moment in a friendly and civil way. It is nice to talk to them, but the boundary there is strong. They are not allowed access close into our life. Unless our friendly acquaintance grows into a casual friendship.

- **Casual friends**. These are people we enjoy the company of when we are with them, but we do not make time for them, they do not make time for us. When we are together, we are friends. These could be co-workers, or people we talk with every year at a specific event, or people we chat with every Sunday morning at church. Casual friends are people we do not really know all that well, so we do not expose our vulnerabilities or our wounds to them. We do not have a history of them demonstrating that they are safe. They are fun to spend time with, but we do not share deeply with them. Maybe they are somebody we have decided will never be more than a casual friend because we hear how they talk about other people. Their talk sounds a little disrespectful and we know that they are likely talking about us in that same way to other people. So we keep them at arm's length. We do not let them into our life closely. We do not share vulnerable information with them. We can stay friendly with them, in their place. Unless we grow in friendship with them and then they may become good friends.

- **Good friends.** Of these, we could have about a dozen or so. We make time for each other; we go to events together and share meals together. Every month, we make time to enjoy each other's company. Good friends are the people who get fairly close to us. They do not know everything about our life, but they knew know us pretty well and we know them pretty well. We regularly spend time together and we grow together doing things that are beneficial for each of us. These are people that we can talk to about a lot of the things that we are thinking about in life. These are people who have demonstrated over time that they care about us that they allow us to care about them. They would not use anything that they know about us to hurt us. Some of these people may develop into our best friends.

- **The best of friends**, the ones we really need in our life, are usually 3 or 4 really close friends. These people who know us well, support us, and encourage us. They are people we can turn to when we are stressed or in trouble and they will help us. We can share our joys with them and they with delight in our happiness. We make time for these people generally every week. We talk and we meet regularly. The very best of friends are often people that live close to us. But even when they may be far away we can intentionally choose to keep the closeness of this relationship. They are safe people who know a lot about us, and we know a lot about them. They have demonstrated that they are trustworthy, that they will not use the information they know about us—the vulnerabilities that we have—to hurt us. These are the people who help us to grow into the people we are designed to be. They will not help us to do wrong. They are loyal to us, but they are more loyal to the core of our shared values, and that is beneficial to us. These people know us well enough, care about us well enough, and love us enough to call us on our stuff when we are doing things that are wrong. They compassionately speak the truth to us.

Friends are vital connections in our lives. Friends are the family that we choose. In order to keep good friendships we have to develop and maintain them.

In general, we all were born into a family, a tribe, a people. We were born in a place among others also born there. These are the ones we started our connections with. Inherently, we know that we need to belong somewhere. In the best case, these connections are nurturing, kind people who help you to grow and mature.

*Walk with the wise and become wise,*
*for a companion of fools suffers harm.*
*Proverbs 13:20*

Sometimes the people you were born to may have their own struggles with growing and maturing. Perhaps they do not know how to set boundaries for themselves nor how to respect other people's boundaries. Sometimes it is helpful for your own growth to limit the interactions you have with people who have unsafe behaviors.

*Do not make friends with a hot-tempered person,*
*do not associate with one easily angered,*
*or you may learn their ways*
*and get yourself ensnared.*
*Proverbs 22:24-25*

You can find a healthy set of people to be a part of. In Christ, we are to love one another. Within the people who know, love, and follow Jesus, you can connect to safe people, creating your own set of family, people, tribe, the ones you choose. However, not everyone who calls themselves a Christian is safe. A lot of Christians, no matter what their chronological age, are young and still maturing in their faith. They may be an older person and yet still figuring out how to heal and grow, still figuring out how to have healthy boundaries. You have to look to find healthy people to connect with. The healthiest people are the ones who recognize their own need to heal and grow. You pour into them, and they into you. They need you as much as you need them.

## In summary

We all need connections. It is important to our own growth, healing, and happiness. We were born into our first connections. As we grow and mature, we choose our own connections. Being connected to people with healthy, safe boundaries is important.

# CHAPTER 8

## Being a Safe Person

People with healthy, safe boundaries and behaviors like to connect to other people with healthy, safe boundaries and behaviors. Being a safe person is a learned skill. Part of being a safe person is a choice of our will to do what's in the best interest of the other person. That assumes you are paying enough attention to the other person that you know what they might need. For example: you pay attention to the other drivers on the road, to the other people who might walk through the park, the other people at the campground, and the other people you are around at home and at work. Safe people do not make life harder for other people; we try to make it better for people.

The truth is, we have all behaved thoughtlessly and unkindly at some time in our lives. We have all hurt others. Sometimes it was unconsciously done other times it was a result of our upbringing and environment. Sometimes it may have been a deliberate choice. Not matter the why or how or our past it was behavior that can damage connections. Becoming a safe person nearly all the time takes effort and is a learned skill. You can become a safe person even if you have not been one before. Here are some commonly agreed on characteristics of "safe" people.

## Characteristics of safe people

- People who listen to you without judging you, even when they do not agree.
- People who are able to validate your right to your feelings and just listen, without trying to fix everything,
- People who are kind and behave kindly to others.
- People who accept that no one is perfect and have grace for imperfections.
- People who can stay neutral, letting you talk things out.
- People who are loyal to truth and can confront gently with compassion.
- People who are patient and take time to get to know you, letting you get to know them.
- People who encourage you to grow, ones who are a good influence on you.
- People who can be respectfully intimate and not enmeshed.
- People who see all others as people of value, due respect.
- People who are honest and keep their word.
- People who are okay with silence.

These are some common characteristics of safe people. There are others, but this will give you an idea of the attitudes and behaviors of safe people. Now let's look at some of the common characteristics of unsafe behaviors and attitudes that people have.

## Characteristics of unsafe behaviors and attitudes

- An attitude of self-righteousness and acting like they have it all together.
- Treating others like they are less valuable and less worthy of respect.
- Demanding trust and intimacy without it being earned.
- Wanting their own needs met but having little or no regard for the needs of others.
- Controlling, manipulative, abusive.
- Defensive, not open to constructive feedback.
- Unreliable, not trustworthy, deceptive
- Apologizing, but not changing behavior.
- Blaming others and not take responsibility for own stuff.
- Hanging on to bitterness and holding grudges.
- Not caring about others and their needs.
- Not growing, keeping same unhealthy patterns of behavior.

The truth is, we have all had unsafe attitudes or behaviors in our lives. We have all hurt others. Becoming a safe person takes a deliberate choice and then the effort to examine our own attitudes and behaviors, assessing what we need to change to become safer. It is a learned skill. You can become a safe person.

## How to Become a Safe Person

- Ask for help. The people around you have seen and experienced your unsafe behaviors, so they can help you assess what would be good to change. Asking requires humility on your part and the safe attitude of being willing to take constructive feedback with grace.
- Avoid excusing your past behaviors. Instead, focus on moving toward change. Take ownership of the truth of your past unsafe attitudes. Ask for forgiveness.
- Express your desire to let them know they matter to you, you care about them, that you will not reject them. Ask for the assurances you need as you work through this process.
- Work through your own tendency to avoid growth. Be open to truth.
- Learn how to accept forgiveness and to give forgiveness.

We all need to help others and be helped by others. That is a healthy part of growing deeply connected. A safe person knows deeply about you and would never use that information to hurt you, but rather helps you to grow.

## Fruit of the Spirit

Safe people demonstrate the fruit of the spirit. It makes connections stronger and flow more easily.

*But the fruit of the Spirit is*
*love, joy, peace, forbearance,*
*kindness, goodness, faithfulness,*
*gentleness and self-control.*
*Against such things there is no law.*
*Galatians 5:22, 23*

- **Love** seeks the welfare of the other. It is an unselfish loyal and benevolent concern for the good of another, to do what is in the long-term best interest of another. A choice of will.
- **Joy** is a deep welling of contentment and gladness in the Lord that is not dependent upon our circumstances. Joy is there even in the midst of troubles. Joy is a stronger, more lasting feeling than happiness.
- **Peace** is a state of being sound and complete. Having harmony and wholeness. The absence of strife or war. To make amends and put things right.
- **Forbearance** is patience; the ability to calmly accept or tolerate difficulties or annoying people, situations, tasks, troubles; or suffering without getting angry or upset. It is being willing to wait pleasantly and with a good attitude.
- **Kindness** is to show consideration toward others, to be aware of their needs, to have a good nature or disposition, to be helpful and caring about other people.
- **Goodness** is the deliberate preference of right to wrong, the firm and persistent resistance of all moral evil, and the choosing and following of all moral good.

- **Faithfulness** means to be firm in adherence to promises or in observance of duty; steadfast in affection or allegiance, true to the facts, to a standard, or to an original. Someone who is consistent and reliable; they are true to their word. Someone you can depend on to do what is right.
- **Gentleness** is the soft touch of a strong hand. It is kind and considerate of others; a humble, compassionate, and tender approach to the weakness and limitations of others.
- **Self-control** is the ability to control oneself; to regulate behaviors, emotions, and the way they are expressed, especially in difficult situations; the ability to not do the things that your feelings make you want to do, altering your responses to work toward your long-term goals; to have your strength under control.

### Each Carry Your Own Load

A safe person looks around to see the effect they are having on the world. We can pick up our own messes, clean up our own dishes, and pick up our own clothes so that other people don't have to clean up after us. Carrying your own load makes you easy to be around. You don't drain other people's energy.

When we go to parks and stores and we leave the place the same quality of cleanliness or better than it was when we came, we are demonstrating safe behavior. A safe person does not make other people's lives harder. They are aware of what other people need and how can they make life better for the people around them. Oftentimes, we can do just little bits of things that make life easier for people. We can appreciate the things that they do for us and tell them that.

Think about how many public parks and campgrounds and streets littered with garbage people have just thrown down. That is an example of making life harder for other people. It is a symptom of unsafe behavior. It demonstrates that, since I do not want to have to deal with this trash, I will just drop it wherever and not think about it. Somebody else is paid to clean that up anyway.

That kind of careless attitude can carry over into many other parts of life. Those unsafe behaviors demonstrate a lack of care that they are making life harder for other people. Is it a sense of cluelessness, never having learned responsibility? Or is it that they think other people should always do things for them and it is a sense of entitlement? That type of entitlement is not a part of safe behaviors. Safe people demonstrate responsible behaviors.

Being a Good Visitor

*Seldom set foot in your neighbor's house—*
*too much of you, and they will hate you.*
*Proverbs 25:17*

When you visit, leave people wanting more. Do not use up all your welcome. To be a safe person, we need to respect other people's time. Safe people understand that we cannot be with other people all the time, or they get tired of us. When we go visit our friends and leave while they are still wanting us to stay, we are not using up all of our welcome. That makes them pleased to have us visit again. Anytime they have to give you hints, subtle and not so subtle, to tell you it is time for you to go, you have overstayed your welcome. If every time you visit you overstay your welcome, your friends are not as eager to have you over the next time. They feel like will they enjoy your company, but you will hang around too long when they need to go to bed or go do something else. This makes them reluctant to invite you over.

Instead, when you receive an invitation you can ask then what the ending time is. Also at the event, pay attention to the cues your friends give you. Look at the time when you need to. If you get one hint that it is time to go, acknowledge this and take your leave. It is better to leave when they are still enjoying your presence, rather than stay until they are tired of you. That way they may always be glad to see you.

### In Summary

We all can learn how to be safer with each other. Being a safe person is a learned skill. We can learn to recognize unsafe attitudes and behaviors in ourselves and others. We do not have to stay closely connected with people who choose to stay unsafe.

# CHAPTER 9

---

## Finding that Special Someone

### We All Want to Love and Be Loved.

Finding that someone special to spend your life with is a goal that may take some time and effort. But because this person will be so important to the rest of your life, it is well worth thinking through who you are looking for and the characteristics that are most important to you. Your future happiness depends a lot on your prayerful patience and the quality of your choice.

### Who Are You Looking for?

Are you looking for Miss Perfect? Waiting for Prince Charming? I have bad news for you—Miss Perfect is only looking for Mr. Perfection. Is that you? If not, you are out of luck with her. Waiting for Prince Charming? He married Cinderella eons ago. Out of luck there, too. So, who are you looking for?

*Imagine an old couple in a park. They are walking comfortably together at the same pace. They are holding hands. He points at a tree; she looks at what he is showing her, and they lean together sharing a soft conversation. You can tell from their attitudes that these old people have spent a lifetime together, enjoying each other in happy times, supporting each other in the midst of troubling times, cherishing each other.*

It can take a lot of looking to find that special someone who you could have a committed relationship with. How do you find them? But it is not the first question. The first question is, what do you want? Do you actually want a committed, loving relationship, someone to spend your life with? Or are you looking for any person who may met your needs right now? If you are not in a place where you are looking for a long-term commitment, it is good to acknowledge that and focus on your own character. This chapter is for those who want someone to spend their life with, a committed relationship.

The second consideration is finding someone with whom you share core values. There are a lot of values we can change, or compromise on, but our core values are the most tightly held aspects of who we are and if we try to compromise on those, we can find ourselves in anguish, severe suffering.

Having shared values gives you a solid core to work from as you develop your relationship with this other person. Therefore, an important part of this looking for your special someone is knowing what your most important core values are. I am not talking about the peripheral values that you may compromise on. Those may ebb and flow, growing more together over time. I am talking about your core values.

If the things you hold dear are not shared with a life partner, you are committing your life to someone who is pulling you away from your core values, not helping you to grow toward your core values. That sets you and them up for a life of pain. The challenges of life tend to drive you apart, not drive you together. Sharing the most important values gives you a solid core from which to face the joys and struggles of life together.

Other strongly held values, outside of your core values, are the values that you can discuss and explore and may find ways to navigate through together coming to a consensus, compromise or agreeing to disagree and respect each other's need for that value.

What is it like to share your life with someone who loves you, feels joy in being with you, is peaceful, and has patience with your struggles? Someone who is kind to you, someone who seeks what is good for you, whose faithfulness you can rely on, a strong, gentle person who has self-control? Does that sound like someone you could love? No one has all of these fruits of the spirit fully developed, but many people are committed to growing more and more into these core values.

So when you're thinking of looking for that special someone, sharing core values is important. These core values become your decision-making template of when you meet people. Are they possibly on that track to see if you can develop a good friendship with them? Are they further down your friendship levels without a good chance of moving up? Or could you potentially see yourself developing a lifetime relationship with them?

*Happiness is being married to your best friend.*

Being friends with someone before a committed relationship is an important aspect of a happy partnership. The characteristics of a good friend are vital to a committed relationship. We can have lots of friends, and we need some really good close friends. But we only have one committed spouse. That special one is likely to come from our friend group.

The third important aspect to consider after making the list of what you are looking for is to ask yourself what would a person who has a lot of the characteristics you want be looking for in a person? What do they want? Perhaps they also want someone with those same characteristics. Do you have those characteristics? Are you working on developing those characteristics?

Our core values rarely change as we get older. In fact, they become more mature and more deeply held. When you search for someone you can grow into a better relationship with, if you are searching only for outward physical appearance, you may miss somebody who has those wonderful internal values you treasure.

When you are you shopping for a spouse, what are the characteristics of the person you are looking for? Then think about where a person like that would be. If you are looking for someone who is caring and compassionate, they might be volunteering. When you are looking at places to volunteer, find ones where you are volunteering with a group. Perhaps the person you are looking for is a fellow volunteer or the friend or relative of a fellow volunteer. Look at the friends you have been developing, friends you can trust. Your friends have friends, and your friends have relatives and amongst those people you may find someone.

When you find someone you are interested in getting to know better, social proof is a good step. Go with this person to meet their connections. How do they behave around their family and friends? How do their family and friends treat them? What seems to be their reputation about these people? Take them to meet your family and friends. Let them see how you act around the people you are the most comfortable with. Let them see how you respond to various people that area a part of your history and your current life. You will learn a lot about each other during this process.

If they do not want to share that part of their life with you, that tells you something important about this person. What is hidden, why is it hidden? Are they ashamed of you? Are they ashamed of where they come from? Why do they not have friends to share? These are important questions.

## Premarital Counseling

Many couples find great value in premarital counseling. The purpose is to find your areas of strengths so you can use those resources to grow in your relationship. Also to find areas of differences so that those can be intentionally addressed to avoid future relationship struggles. This vital counseling helps to get your relationships off on a solid footing as you move forward in your new life together.

## In Summary

We all want to love and be loved. Finding that someone special to spend your life with is a goal that may take some time and effort. But because this person will be so important to the rest of your life, it is well worth thinking through your own core values and the characteristics you want in a life partner. Your future happiness depends a lot on your prayerful patience in this endeavor.

# CHAPTER 10

## Healthy, Committed Relationship

An older couple was telling their Sunday morning group at church about their weekend. These two people were in their mid-eighties. They had celebrated their 65th wedding anniversary the day before. He still referred to her as his "bride" in a tone of voice that let you know he cherishes this woman. She called him by name, and you could see the light of love shining in her eyes. He told us about a phone call he had with his mother-in-law two days ago. "She said to me, 'Now Johnny, you take her somewhere real nice for dinner.'" We laughed with him at the tone and happiness he related in the story, while we were wondering, how old must his mother-in-law be? She must be about a hundred years old!

As I thought about this couple, I remembered the easy grace they had in each other's company. They often held hands as they walked together. You never heard either of them say an unkind or negative comment about each other, or anyone else. They supported and encouraged each other in the stories they told of their fun times together. Individually and together, they always had time to talk with people and to listen and support people around them. They had a reputation of being available and helpful to anyone in need. They each volunteered in different ministries in the church. And they would mentor other couples who were younger than them—which was almost everyone!

They modeled many of the components of a safe, loving, committed relationship:

- Commitment to each other and their marriage
- Loyalty to their shared values
- Loyalty to their spouse in all that is right
- Gently correcting each other in something that is wrong
- Gracefully accepting correction as a loving act
- Genuine enjoyment of each other's company
- Shared interests, time together in shared fun
- Supporting each other in separate interests
- Facilitating a close relationship with the spouse's extended family
- Making time to be alone together to share special moments
- Having time away from each other for separate interests
- Making time to be together with joint friends
- Finding and nurturing joint friends

When we think of this couple, how many of us would like to be in that kind of a loving, committed relationship? Ever wonder what it takes to get there?

This couple was showing the evidence of two people who have worked hard to come to a place of easy comfort with each other. Their relationship did not just happen; they put effort into it so it could grow into that safe haven from the world's struggles.

*Love is patient, love is kind.*
*It does not envy, it does not boast,*
*it is not proud. It is not rude,*
*it is not self-seeking, it is not easily angered,*
*it keeps no record of wrongs.*
*Love does not delight in evil*
*but rejoices with the truth.*
*It always protects, always trusts,*
*always hopes, always perseveres.*
*1 Corinthians 13:4-7*

Once you find that special person and you get married, you start your life together in a honeymoon of bliss. Then you discover they leave dirty dishes in the sink, they throw their socks on the floor, or they don't take out the garbage, or hundred other little things that now irritate you. Having a wonderful marriage is not just finding the person and getting married. Your happiness will rely on how you work out what is important in your family. You work out your family values together, deciding what kind of family you want to be.

When you already agree on the core values, you are able to work through the other values more easily as the two of you meld together into a strong family. It is important to work through the things that keep coming up in arguments. Find how can you resolve that argument, putting it completely to rest so you are not arguing over the same things again and again. Some things you have to make compromises on with some give and take. Sometimes one person makes a sacrifice. Figure out what is more important to one spouse than the other. Be careful not to take advantage of declaring something is important when it is just a preference.

*I just want a person*
*who is more interested in me*
*than they are in themselves*
*but more interested in "us"*
*than they are in me.*

There are some things that you can grow together and some things we cannot seem to change and therefore we need to adapt to it. We figure out how to adapt in a way that will not be a constant source of irritation. Talk about the attitude and atmosphere we want in our home, building that together makes for a rich homelife. The relationship itself needs to be nurtured so that it can grow together to intimacy.

Areas of intimacy

When we discuss intimacy in a marriage, people often think of just one kind of intimacy—sexual intimacy. However, a good marriage has at least five kinds of intimacy:

1.  Sexual intimacy. Sharing a faithful sexual relationship, a sexual bond.
2.  Physical intimacy. This is different than sexual intimacy. For couples this looks like the hug and quick kiss after work, a squeeze of the hand

when someone walks by, a head on a shoulder while watching a movie

3. Emotional intimacy. Sharing what I feel and how my emotions are affected by what I am experiencing.
4. Intellectual intimacy. Sharing what I am learning, what I know, what I am thinking, my opinions.
5. Spiritual intimacy. Sharing what I believe and how I am growing in my relationship with God.

A good friendship can have four of these intimacies. In a healthy marriage, there are all of these intimacies but the one that is special and cherished to a marriage is sexual intimacy. In a healthy, committed marriage you have the assurance that you can let your heart safely trust in your spouse, as someone who has your best interest in mind; and that you have their best interest in mind. But more than that, they are on the side of truth and what's right and they encourage you toward truth and what's right. They encourage you toward what God wants in your life and then the two of you grow together in your faith and your relationship with each other. Loving and equipping each other for works of service, helping each other to be the best that you can be.

### Areas of Growing Together

Additional areas to be worked through and grow together in include:

- Money—How are the bills going to be handled? How are financial decisions made? What is the amount of money each spouse can spend without consulting the other?

- Conflict—How to fight fair, resolving conflict in a way that respects each person on the family and puts issues to rest.
- Recreational—The time and money spent on recreation. What is done together, what separately?
- Decision making—How are decisions worked through? What are joint decisions? What are individual decisions?

The very process of working through the areas in your marriage can help strengthen your connections if you work through them as safe people, respecting each person's viewpoint as you resolve conflicts.

In Summary

Finding that wonderful significant other is a start, but your happiness depends a lot on how you both do the hard work of growing together in your healthy committed relationship.

# CHAPTER 11

---

## Children

*Children are a heritage from the Lord,*
*offspring a reward from him.*
*Psalm 127:3*

The natural outpouring of many committed relationships is the nurturing of children. Most often these are children who are born to the couple, but it also can include children who are adopted or fostered. Children bring great joy to a marriage, but also stress and struggle. In general, the happiness and joy far outweigh the effort it takes to raise a child.

However, it is important to remember these children are entrusted to your care. Therefore, you want your family to be a safe place for them to be nurtured and grow up. Within that, teach them how to be safe and how to connect with people. Children see what you model. They see how you treat each other and how you treat other people. You can be the generation in your family that teaches your children healthy boundaries, respect, and kindness; nurturing your child helps your child to understand how to love God and to love others.

Children are a blessing. They are entrusted to our care by God. If we start with an attitude that this child is precious and this child is loved, there is nothing that child can do to destroy that love.

Think about a newborn baby, holding the tiny infant in your arms. Does that baby have value? Of course, it does. Yet all that baby does is swallow and eliminate. We understand that the baby has value just because they exist, just because they are human. That value does not rely on anything that a child does or doesn't do, or anything that happened to them or did not happen to them. All humans have that inherent value just because we exist. We are valuable and worthy of dignity and respect, and nothing can destroy that value. Nothing the child has done can destroy that value, nothing that anybody did to the child can destroy that value because they did not do anything to get that value.

Your child should know they are safe in your love. No matter how they behave, they are safe in your love. Inappropriate behavior may have consequences, but loss of love is not one of the consequences.

When we first have a child, the parents do everything for the child and the child can do very little for themselves; all they do is swallow and eliminate. But by the time that they are an adult, whatever age that is, we want to equip them to be able to do everything for themselves. In order to do that, each year we

74

review our goals for the child as an adult and decide what we need to teach and equip them this year to keep moving toward that goal.

Some parents might say, "Well, I don't want to push my goals onto my child. I want them to make their own goals." Think about that a little more. Do you want him to live to be an adult? Well, then you have health goals for your child. Would you like her to be able to read, write, spell, and do math? Then you have education goals for your child. Would you like them to be able to be able to get their own food and shelter? That might encompass a few different goals, like learning how to be responsible and hold a job to bring in an income, being able to shop at a grocery store, and learning how to handle money. We all have goals for our children.

Do you want to be in relationship with your child when they are an adult? Then you have social goals, extended family goals. You will become extended family when your child goes off into a life of their own to start their own family. How are you modeling for your child how to interact with extended family now in the way that you treat your extended family? Would you like to be a part of the lives of your grandchildren and see them grow up? That requires that you have a good relationship with your child. There are a lot of goals that every parent has for their child. You are not trying to control your child's life but rather to equip your child with the skills that they need so they can choose their own way. This doesn't mean making all their decisions for them, but training them into how to make good decisions for themselves so they can choose their own way.

Right from the start, you can train your children to be safe people, to have safe behaviors, to respect other people's rights and other people's belongings, and to treat people with dignity. This training involves more than what you tell them. They're going to learn a great deal just by watching you. Little children want to be like mom and dad. You are modeling the values you hold dear. In that modeling, you can show them how to be a safe person from the very start of their life. Other things we teach deliberately and intentionally. As we walk through life with them, we talk about how what we do is in line with our values. When we want to share our values with our children, we both teach and model. They hear us, and they see us live them out.

There is an old saying, "Do as I say, not as I do." The appropriate response to that is, "What you do speak so loud I can't hear what you say." When we want our children to grow up into adults with a safe social community, that starts with the unconditional love they see at home. When a young girl has safe, unconditional love from her dad and then a sweet-talking conman comes by, she is going to recognize the fake that is and not be led away by it. She has experienced the real thing, so fakes are obvious. When you think about what kind of person would you like your child to grow up to be, what kind of values would you like your child to have, ask yourself, "Do I have those values right now? Am I modeling those values to your children daily?"

**In Summary**

The natural outpouring of many committed relationships is the nurturing of children. Children bring great joy to a marriage, along with stress and struggle. In general the happiness and joy far outweighs the effort it takes to raise a child. We review our goals for our children and decide how we need to teach and equip them. Your children want to be like you. In the way you live you show them what is important in life. we both teach and model our values to our children. In nurturing the next generation, you are leaving a deep mark on this world.

# CHAPTER 12

---

## Supporting Connections

We all need more than a relationship with one significant person in our lives. We have our primary relationship, and then there are the supporting connections. If we try to get all of our logistical needs, physical needs, emotional needs, intellectual needs, and friendship needs met through just one person, they can feel like they are drowning or having the life sucked out of them. No one person is going to be able to meet all of your needs. Likewise, you will not be able to meet all the needs of your significant other. We all need supporting connections.

### The richness of diversity

We all need to be connected to a number of people and when we are connected to people who are like us it can feel comfortable and easy. But we also need to be connected to others who are different from us so that we have a richer and more fulfilling, happier life. Diversity is the way life is designed.

*Just as our bodies have many parts and each part has a special function, so it is with Christ's body. We are many parts of one body, and we all belong to each other.*

*In his grace, God has given us different gifts for doing certain things well. So if God has given you the ability to prophesy, speak out with as much faith as God has given you. If your gift is serving others, serve them well. If you are a teacher, teach well. If your gift is to encourage others, be encouraging. If it is giving, give generously. If God has given you leadership ability, take the responsibility seriously. And if you have a gift for showing kindness to others, do it gladly.*

*Don't just pretend to love others. Really love them. Hate what is wrong. Hold tightly to what is good. Love each other with genuine affection, and take delight in honoring each other.*

*Romans 12:4-10*

In the Christian life, we are told we are all parts of one body: we are all different, but all are needed, like eyes, hands, feet, and ears. Like parts of a body are connected to many other parts, we need to be connected to more than one friend. It can be beneficial when those people are different than you. We need people who are like us and understand us, but we also need people who are different than us, so we can broaden our understanding of humanity. It makes a richer life for everybody.

When we have friendships with people who are older than us and younger than us, it helps us to grow. It lets us mentor somebody who is not yet in the stage of life we are and be mentored by someone who has already gone through this stage of life. New parents whose children are infants and toddlers can be mentored by parents of school-age children. Parents of school-age children can be mentored by parents of teenagers. In this, we can see what developmental stage is coming and our mentors can help us with what we are dealing with right now. Having one up and one down relationships enriches our life and the lives of the others we are connected to. These supporting connections in our life are important.

## Neighbors

We also have connections with neighbors. Wherever we live, there are neighbors. Out in the country, the neighbors may be far away; in housing developments, the neighbors are in the house next door; in housing buildings, the neighbors can be on the other side of the wall. Whether near or far, their behavior affects us and our behavior affects them. If we have a conflicted relationship with a neighbor, it makes life harder for them and harder for us. When we get along with our neighbors it makes life easier for them and easier for us.

## 10 Ways to Be a Good Neighbor

Taking the time to know your neighbors makes you feel safer in your community. Sometimes it can be difficult to get along with neighbors, but a good start is to be a good neighbor.

1. Be friendly—You do not have to be best friends with a neighbor, but being friendly includes letting your neighbors know what you like about them: their kindness for example. As a good neighbor, be aware of the ways they are a good neighbor. Share a plate of cookies. It builds goodwill and might even make them feel less lonely.

2. Smile and greet—When you see your neighbor smile, give a simple greeting. Introduce yourself. Learn their names. Smiling and saying "Hi" is easy and can make someone's day. Saying hello helps you earn some benefit toward a closer-knit neighborhood, where others know you and look out for you, increasing safety for everyone.

3. Don't be snoopy or gossipy—It is okay to casually notice what your neighbor is doing. It is not friendly to peer over fences and intently watch and comment on everything a neighbor does.

4. Be responsible for your pets—Don't let your pets be a source of irritation to your neighbors. Don't let your dog relieve themselves on your neighbor's property. Pick up your dog's feces. The smell travels across boundary lines. Don't let your dog's barking annoy your neighbors.

5. Keep your yard tidy—A messy yard is noticed by neighbors and does not please anyone. Good neighbors keep visible spaces such as yard, stoop, garbage cans, or balcony tidy so neighbors don't have to see mess or clutter.

6. Be helpful and don't ask for too many favors— Offer to help lift or carry heavy or awkward things. Be cautious about asking for help. Just because your neighbors live right next door doesn't mean that they want to help you out all the time.

7. Be respectful and give your neighbors some space—Be respectful of your neighbor's privacy and things. Don't visit too often or stay too long.

8. Be a respectful party host—Be aware of the effect your party is having on your neighbors: is the sound traveling to the neighbor? Did your guests park in a way that affects the neighbors? Is your party running late, affecting neighbor's sleep? Are your guests talking loudly as they leave? Sometimes you may be able to invite your neighbors to your party, showing generosity and perhaps getting a little forgiveness for your loud friend.

9. Be quiet—A good neighbor is quiet. Everyone has a right to quiet enjoyment of their own home, including your neighbors. Sound can travel farther than you think. Limit noise and activity that may affect your neighbors, especially during the normal quiet hours of 10:00pm to 7:00 am.

10. Handle conflict judiciously—No matter how friendly you are, you may have conflict with neighbors. Handling conflicts politely is important. The first step is to figure out what part of the problem is your own. Then, generally, if you have an issue with a neighbor, try to resolve the problem with the person

directly. Face to face is most effective. If face to face doesn't work, then try email and posted letters. Your city may also have neutral mediators who can help you resolve disputes.

## Landlords and Tenants

If you rent your home, you have a connection with your landlord. Generally, it is the legal duty of a landlord to provide a dwelling that is fit to live in. It is the legal duty of a tenant to live in a dwelling the way it is supposed to be lived in. The specific legal tenant landlord laws are different in in different localities, so those you would have to look up. What I am discussing is diligence and attitude.

If you are the tenant, treating your landlord with kindness and respect goes a long way toward you having a good experience in your home. Respecting the dwelling includes not damaging the property and not having garbage or clutter build up around the property. You are treating the landlord respectfully when you pay your rent on or before it is due, and you live in a dwelling in the way that a dwelling is meant to be lived in.

If you are the landlord, you can respectfully provide for your tenant a place that is comfortable and fit to live in. You respect their privacy and their needs. When there is a maintenance issue that needs to be done, you do it promptly and cheerfully. Your attitude of kindness and respect goes a long way toward making that connection functional.

## Teachers and Childcare Workers

When you are a parent, you have connections with teachers and childcare workers. When you interact with them in a way that is kind and respectful, it builds connection. These people take care of the most precious thing in your life, so a good connection with them includes treating them with respect and gratefulness for the work that they do and also understanding their responsibilities. Being kind to them includes keeping your child clean and fed. It includes showing up with everything they will need to care for your child and returning to your children on time.

We also have teachers on our parenting team, working with us to equip our children for a competent adulthood. We keep track of what our children are being taught. We oversee our child's homework and talk with their teacher from time to time about their progress.

## Boss and Co-workers

Every boss has a boss. If you are self-employed, every customer is your boss, because you can get fired by every customer. Your connection to your boss will flow better if you are respectful and diligent. Also, your job will be more secure. Be aware of what your boss needs to make the business run productively. What does she need from you? What does the customer need?

When you are the boss, the manager, or supervisor, what do the people who report to you need from you to make their life easier? Whether we are reporting to a boss, the person others report to, or both, when we think wider than our own needs and think of what the needs of the people are around us, our connections work better and everyone's day is easier.

## Governmental Authorities

*Let everyone be subject to the governing authorities, for there is no authority except that which God has established. The authorities that exist have been established by God. Consequently, whoever rebels against the authority is rebelling against what God has instituted, and those who do so will bring judgment on themselves. ... Give to everyone what you owe them: If you owe taxes, pay taxes; if revenue, then revenue; if respect, then respect; if honor, then honor.*

*Romans 13:1-2, 7*

While we are working out how to connect safely with people, let's not forget we have connections to governing authorities. These are the people God put in place to keep this keep the peace and the safety. Each worker in the government is doing their job the best they know how, with the resources that they have and the stresses they have. When you interact with them, take a moment to think about what their day is like and what do they need to make their life a little easier in their interaction with you. The number one thing is about your attitude. Coming to them with a respectful attitude, even a grateful attitude, that somebody is doing that job, then providing all the information that they need, in the way that they need it, so that they don't have extra work, makes a difference in how you are treated. Maybe you had to wait a long time in a line or on a phone call or something before you could get to them. When you finally get to that worker, being kind and polite will make your connection flow better. Don't gripe to them about how long you waited, but just to go on with what you need. When they are through helping you, thank them.

## In Summary

We have our primary relationships, and then there are the supporting connections. We all need supporting connections beyond family and friends. Treating these connections with respect and kindness makes everyone's life better and will help you with what you need in life.

# PART THREE

## Connections Disrupted - Abuse and Safety

In this book we've gone over a lot of information about healthy connections with self and others. This section of the book is about the ways those healthy connections may be disrupted. Many people have not had the luxury of having healthy connections in the past or even the luxury of growing up in a healthy, safe home. This section explores how connections are disrupted and ways that effects our ability to be safe and connect with others.

# CHAPTER 13

## Healthy Connections vs. Abusive Interactions

When healthy connections are disrupted, it creates chaos and harm. Healthy connections are where both parties can get their needs met while respecting the rights and needs of the other. In abusive interactions, one party wants to get their wants met without regard for the rights or needs of the other person and without regard for their harmful effects on the victim. All forms of abuse are illegal in the United States—physical abuse, emotional abuse, spiritual abuse, verbal abuse, sexual abuse, mental abuse, and financial abuse. Everyone has the right to be safe in relationships.

What an abuser wants is control. Sometimes the abuser gets a perverted pleasure in causing hurt to others and seeing others in pain. There is evil in the world. But more often, an abuser is someone who has not learned how to interact in a healthy way, and they are trying to get their own needs met and yet are doing it in a way that drives away the healthy connections they need to meet their needs. Let's explore the differences between healthy connection and abusive interactions.

## Healthy Connection vs Abusive Interactions

- **Healthy connections** are kind, respectful, and empower another person to recognize and celebrate their own potential. Healthy connections recognize and protect each person's freedom to make their own choices.
- **Abusive interactions** are any action that intentionally harms or injures another person in any way. An abusive situation is where one person is seeking the power to control the other through force, intimidation or coercion.

## Healthy vs Abusive Physical Contact.

Physical contact is any person-to-person physical touching or the use of another object to touch a person.

- **Healthy Connection** of physical contact is polite and respectful, making contact with permission, or with minimum necessary touch. One removes touch as soon as the other person gives the slightest indication they do not want the contact.
- **Awkward, Uncomfortable Contact** is when there is non-consensual touch and when people cross boundaries. Maybe they stand too close to you, or their touch may linger after you have indicated you don't want to be touched. This can be cluelessness, or rude.

- **Physical abuse** is touching someone inappropriately, hitting, punching, grabbing a person, or restraining them so they cannot leave. Physical abuse includes an injury that is inflicted by non-accidental means that results in harm.

## Dependent-specific Abuse

We have a duty to do what is in the best interest of those entrusted to our care, especially children or vulnerable adults.

- **Healthy connection** is demonstrated by parents who nurture and protect their children, providing not only for a child's physical needs of shelter, food, medical care, and supervision, but also for mental and emotional needs.
- **Neglect** is failure through action or lack of action to provide and maintain food, shelter, medicine, supervision, protection, or nurturance to such a degree that a person's health and safety are endangered. Particularly a child or a vulnerable adult.

## Safety and Protection

- **Healthy connections** provide safety and protection, especially for children or vulnerable adults entrusted to their care. Safety is a confidence in the freedom from risk of harm, injury, or danger. Protection is the steps to be taken by those with the duty, power, or responsibility to ensure safety.
- **Threat of harm** is making verbal or physical threats of harm. And for children, threat of

harm includes witnessing or intervening in domestic violence or subjecting a child to severe harm of physical abuse, sexual abuse, neglect, mental injury, or other child abuse or neglect.

## Nurturing

- **Healthy nurturing** is to enjoy gentle ways to make others feel good, cared about, encouraged, and comforted, so that other people feel safe to be who they are in your presence.
- **Emotional or Mental Injury** is continuing pattern of rejecting, terrorizing, ignoring, isolating, or corrupting a child, resulting in serious mental or emotional damage to adult or a child.

## Sexual Interaction

Sexual interaction is any contact physically, visually, or audibly designed to arouse sexual feelings or responses in another.

- **Healthy sexual interaction** is between two adults who both have consented, every single time, with mutually understandable permission, given by words or actions, regarding one's willingness to engage in sexual activity. They generally have mutual pleasure-giving in mind.
- **Sexual abuse and sexual exploitation** is forcing sexual contact without consent to a person of any age. Any sexual contact in which a child or teen younger than 18 years is used to sexually stimulate another person is illegal. This may be

anything from rape to fondling to involving a child in pornography.

What an abuser gains is a temporary fulfillment of a need. What an abuse victim loses is a long-term trust in people, damage to sense of self and emotional wounds that linger and negatively affect their connections with others for years to come. The victim experiences years or a lifetime of trauma effects.

The abuser wants to break the connections of the victim, get them separated from any resources, until they are helpless and alone. It is easier for the abuser to control the victim when they separate them from resources. One of the first resources they are trying to separate them from is other connections in their life: family, extended family, friends, and even coworkers. Abusers work to erode or break those connections in a lot of different ways, some subtle and some blatant. They may talk about negatively about "those" people, how they don't like those people, and the victim shouldn't like them either because they are not good people. They point out all the flaws they have and how they are uncomfortable around them and say something like, "If you loved me you wouldn't want me to have to be around those people."

Abusers also hinder the victim from contacting or being with those people without the abuser. Another way they do it is by interfering with the time that would be spent with those people. Any time that might be spent with supportive connections, something comes up were the abuser wants to be with the victim and so there isn't time for them to be with anyone else.

The effect of that is that their time to be with family and friends gets diminished.

Another way that time is broken into is that the abuser makes demands. For example, the house needs to be cleaned, the yard has to be done, or the abuser's clothes or food need to be taken care of. Abusers put all these kind of barriers in the way so there isn't time for the victim to be with their family and friends. In all of these ways, and many others, an abuser tries to erode or break the connections that a victim has with their other connections or any source of resources so the victim won't have somebody who can help them out of the life of abuse. The result is the victim becomes totally dependent on the abuser for resources.

There is evil in the world. Some people have chosen to be evil and get pleasure out of controlling and hurting others. However, other people grew up in an abusive environment and they considered these patterns of behavior as normal in their world. The modeling they saw about how people interact, how anger is handled and how frustration is expressed was abusive, controlling, and disrespectful. As a child they accepted these behaviors as the way life was. Just as an abused victim may accept abuse as an adult because they think it is the way life is.

But as people grow older and mature, they begin to make their own choices about how to interact with others. Other models exist in schools, on media, etc. that are there and show a different way to live. Surviving abuse is not a justifiable excuse for continuing the cycle as an abuser.

## Whose Fault and Whose Responsibility

How someone was treated as a child is not their fault; however, it is that person's responsibility what kind of adult they choose to become. When they bump into a person with boundaries, they may try to push the boundaries because it the way they know. When the boundary is held firm, they have a choice to make: respect the boundary and learn new healthy ways of interacting or go more toward dysfunction and continually try to cross the boundary or to break off relationships and go away from the person with boundaries.

## Dance of Change

When you decide to make a change, you will affect those close to you. Relationships can be like a dance. Both of you know the steps and how the dance usually goes. Each time one person moves, the other person has to move to stay in step. When one of you decides to make a change, when one of you decides to heal and grow healthy, it will affect the other. The first response the other makes is to try to pull you back into the same dance, to get you back into step with the dance they know. If you will not be pulled back into that unhealthy dance, they have a choice to make. They either have to pull away and leave the dance, or they have to change to learn how to stay in step with you in this new dance. It is their choice.

If they choose to start changing and to learn the new dance, the connection grows because now both people are working toward making this a healthy connection.

## Healthy Connections

People in healthy relationships support each other to have healthy outside connections. Healthy people facilitate ways for people to connect and keep strong connects with other people. They facilitate family connections, extended family connections, and friendship connections for their spouse because they want their spouse to have what they need. Healthy people know that we are we are created to be connected to people and we need connections to more than one person. If in the extended family there are some people that that aren't healthy and are detrimental or even abusive, they may support their spouse by being with them on the few times they need to be around that person, like a family gathering. Then they can stay connected with the healthy people in the family and they are supported as well as protected from being alone with abusive people.

People in healthy relationships work together at having couple friends that they can see together and enjoy together, but they also support each other in having individual friends. When you are in a faithful relationship, it doesn't threaten somebody to have their partner be friends with somebody else or doing an activity with a friend. The partners each make sure that they are faithful and straightforward and open about where they are, who they are with, and what they are doing at any time. There is no there is no cause for jealousy and there is no jealousy because their hearts are faithful to each other. Healthy relationships support and encourage independence and interdependence, but not dependence.

## Types of Dependence

- **Dependence** is the state of relying on, being controlled by, or being influenced by someone or something else for aid, support, or the like.
- **Independence** is freedom from dependence; being free from reliance on or control by others; being able to maintain one's own self without interference.
- **Interdependence** describes a relationship in which each person depends on the other; they can rely on each other. They have both freedom and support.

## In Summary

Healthy connections are where both parties can get their needs met while respecting the boundaries, rights, and needs of the other. In abusive interactions, one party wants to get their wants met without regard to the rights or needs of the other person and without regard to the harmful effects on the victim. When boundaries are constantly violated, healthy connections are disrupted, and it creates chaos and harm. Change is possible, but not everyone chooses to change.

# CHAPTER 14

## Abuse, Manipulation, Guilt

When we see or experience boundaries that are constantly crossed, when we are treated disrespectfully, that may be abuse. When things are not going the way we want, it is normal for intense feelings to be triggered. It is normal to feel angry about the violation. Anger is not wrong; it is not a sin. Feeling angry, hurt, or afraid is normal. Feelings are okay; feelings just happen. But behavior is always a choice—bad behavior is NOT OKAY.

### The Manipulation of Abuse

People have free will and get to choose how to behave. Sometimes people make unsafe choices. All of us make unsafe choices once in a while, but some people make unsafe choices all the time. They use their free will to hurt themselves and to hurt and abuse others.

Abusive control doesn't have to be physical. It can also be through manipulation and the use of guilt. If the goal is to control another person's behavior to the benefit of the abuser, it is abuse. The abuser wants what they want with little or no regard to how that is affecting other people. They have no respect for other people's rights or boundaries. And yet, at times, they may not even be aware they are behaving abusively. When a person is raised within a family or family system where abuse is the norm, they may not be aware that their behavior is abusive.

I'm not talking here about physical violence: any healthy person should be any person should be aware that physical violence to other people is wrong. Here what I'm talking about is how some people grow up in a household where, for instance, people don't make clear statements. Instead they manipulate or talk around things or try to get other people to get other people to do what they want instead of clearly and directly asking for what they want.

Manipulation includes trying to triangle others into our conversations and behaviors to try to gain other support for what we want. Triangulation is an unhealthy manipulation tactic where one person will not communicate directly with another person, instead they try to use a third person to relay communication to the second, thus forming a triangle.

Healthy interactions include clear and direct communication with the person we need to have communication with, not asking someone else to do it for us, or complaining to someone who has no power or authority to change what we want changed. When we complain to the wrong people or in the wrong way, we have little chance of getting the result we want, and we are gossiping and spreading discord among others. So they continue to try to guilt somebody into doing something for them instead of just asking and accepting no when somebody says no. This has a negative effect on relationships. It is an unhealthy and perhaps abusive way to behave.

**There is another choice.**

When we say no to a request we are demonstrating a boundary we have set up in our own life. We can expect that people are going to push our boundaries, it is how they find the edge of the boundary. Boundaries define what is mine and not mine. What we are responsible for and what we are not responsible for. Good boundaries define how close I let other people get in my life. When we have healthy boundaries, we can risk getting close to some people and letting some people get close to us. When we have experienced betrayal, abuse, bullying, or trauma as a child, we may never have been allowed to develop boundaries or had our boundaries respected. While we yearn for connection with people, we know that people can hurt us. The world can feel unsafe. We may bounce back and forth between trusting people too much and getting hurt again to trusting no one and being isolated and alone.

Setting healthy boundaries is what allows us to develop healthy relationships with people. We can set up how far we let people have access to our lives. We let them in a little way and see how they behave. Those who are respectful, we may let in closer. When we set up our boundaries and refuse to let anyone cross them, we're teaching the people in our lives how to treat us more respectfully. When someone wants to guilt us into doing something for them, remember it's just an *offer* of guilt. We do not have to accept it. You can look at it and ask if it is your guilt to own. Is it true? If we have done something we are guilty of, we do want to repair it and to ask for forgiveness for it. But sometimes it's not true guilt someone is trying to give you. It's a false guilt—a sense of manipulation. That's an unsafe way for people to behave and we do not have to accommodate that.

I get to choose when my body is touched

Sometimes somebody will try to guilt you into allowing more physical connection. They will say, "If you really love me, you'll do this." Actually, if someone really loved you, they wouldn't ask you to do that. Sex without consent is never okay. Touching without consent is crossing a boundary, too. These are unsafe behaviors.

Some parents tell their children to go hug a person. The child may not want to hug that person at that time, and yet their parents force them to do that. That is crossing that child's boundary. Behavior can be suggested or encouraged by saying something like, "Would you like to hug that person?" But it should never be forced. When you force a child to touch or hug someone when they don't want to, you are training your child that their "No" has no value when it comes to who touches them and how. The child is also being taught that they are not allowed to have boundaries. Each individual knows who they want to hug, or they don't want to hug, or if they want a hug in a given moment.

Difference between getting kicked or being stumbled over

People are going to bump into our boundaries; it's a normal part of life. Sometimes they don't realize you have a boundary there. When somebody bumps into your boundary, you do not have to take offense at the behavior. We can politely state our boundary and that their behavior was not okay with us, not rejecting the person, just maintaining our boundary. It is okay to say, "No, I choose not to answer that question," or, "No, I don't want to be touched right now," or, "No, I'm not going to give that information." The people who care about us will easily learn that there is a boundary there and they will respect it. However, people who make a habit of unsafe choices and unsafe behaviors may be offended by your boundary. They may continue to push you with demands or guilt. "Well why can't you do this for me?" " I need you to do this for me." "I want you to do this for me anyway." "You have to tell me!" They constantly push against your boundary.

They say even a dog knows the difference between being kicked or getting stumbled over. When people bump into our boundaries or stumble over them, we can calmly let them know we have a boundary here. But some people knowingly kick against our boundaries. They get to choose to push our boundaries, and we get to choose what kind, if any, of relationship we want to maintain with someone who chooses to not respect our boundaries.

## In Summary

All of us make unsafe choices once in a while, but some people make unsafe choices a lot of the time and abuse others. Abusive control may be physical, or through manipulation or guilt. The abuser's goal is to control another person's behavior to the benefit of the abuser. The abuser disregards how that is affecting other people. Having strong boundaries is what allows us to develop healthy relationships with people. Those who are respectful, we may let in closer. When we set up and maintain our boundaries we are teaching the people in our lives how to treat us more respectfully.

# CHAPTER 15

## Why People Stay in Abusive Relationships

Even when a person recognizes they are in an abusive relationship, they may stay in that situation. There are a number of reasons people may stay in abusive relationships. But first let's look at why people may become abusive.

### Why Do People Become Abusive?

We all have needs; to be connected to people, to feel like we have significance, to feel like we are important, to be part of a tribe, group, or community of people. All people are trying to get their needs met. When people did not learn how to connect to others in healthy ways to get these needs met, they may grasp for them in ways that are abusive because that is what they experienced and saw modeled.

Abuse can often come out of insecurities; people have unmet needs, and the models they saw of how to handle that was to manipulate, demand or be aggressive. To be honest, open and request what they need feels vulnerable, they may be afraid to risk that level of vulnerability. But at some point, they are making a conscious choice to try to get what they want through abusive means, even though they know it is detrimental to somebody else.

What happens to them if they stay on that pathway? If they continue to make those abusive choices, they are on a downward spiral. In order to get their needs met, they have to be more and more intense and controlling because they feel like they're losing their control. This downward spiral can lead them to violence that may put them in prison. They may end up killing the person they think they love because they are going on that downward abusive path.

### Why Don't the Victims Leave?

When we recognize that we all have needs, the victims have these same needs of connection. We deeply desire to be connected to others. When we have not experienced healthy connections we may stay in relationships that have components that seem familiar; even if it is abusive. When they begin to find the abuse intolerable there are many reason they may stay.

### Fear of physical harm.

Fear that the abuser may harm them if they try to leave, or that the abuse will get worse if they try to leave and the abuser stops them, is a common reason. This is often a very real risk. Domestic violence is a danger in our society.

### Fear of not being able to make it on their own.

The abuser is the one controlling resources, and if they leave, they don't have any resources. They may never have handled resources on their own and do not know how to get a job, handle income, get housing, or other basic skills of life.

### Fear of losing contact with or custody of their children.

They may have been threatened that that they will never see their kids again if they leave. This connects with having no resources to care for their children on their own, and therefore fear that they are unlikely to be able to get custody.

### A freeze response

There is more than fight or flight responses to high stress. It can be fight, flight, freeze, or submit. A freeze response means they are unable to move in any direction to find help or relief. It can happen in a stressful threat situation.

### A lack of self-esteem

When self-esteem has been eroded over time, it can leave the victim in an uncertain confusion. They have a hard time seeing any options and they don't know what to do or where to go to get help. They may not realize help even exists or that they deserve help.

### Shame at being in the situation

They may think, "I'm the one who caused this. I put myself in this situation. I'm guilty, I'm responsible. Nobody's going to help me because it's all my fault."

That sense of false guilt makes it hard for some victims to reach out and ask for any help.

## The fear of being alone

They long for love and connection. They haven't learned how to be a good friend to themselves. They feel like they have no value unless someone wants them. They need another person to tell them that they are okay, to tell them that life is all right and they're going to make it through.

## Relationship addiction

For some people, toxic relationships can be like being addicted to a substance—but the addiction is to relationships. To have anybody is better than to have nobody. They want to be in a relationship in the worst way. The trouble with that attitude is that sometimes what they end up in a relationship IN THE WORST WAY. They have not yet realized that there is something worse than no relationship: being in an abusive relationship.

## Avoiding acknowledgement of another failure

Some abuse victims stay because to leave the abusive situation they would have to accept that it is another failed relationship, and they feel grief about that. They don't want to lose that ideal in their mind that this was going to be a wonderful relationship. It was going to fix all the things heartache in their life, but it's not the reality that they're living.

## Having hope

The abuser says they are sorry, says it will never happen again. The victim has hope that this time that will be true. They may also have hope that if they could just be the person the abuser tells them they need to be, the abuser will change, and this relationship will become ideal.

## Having no hope

Conversely, maybe they think all relationships are abusive. Some victims stay in an abusive relationship because they have no hope that there is any other kind of life available. At least the way this one is abusive is familiar to them. The chaos, arguing, and fighting may be familiar to the victim, so common that they know it and may even think they are comfortable with it.

## Peace feels uncomfortable

When they are in a relationship without those elements of drama, chaos, and abuse, they can feel anxious because drama has been their normal lifestyle. The unknown feelings of peace feel scary, and they tell themselves they are uncomfortable. But uncomfortable is not the same thing as unfamiliar. They are actually experiencing something they have not known or don't recognize, something they don't have knowledge or experience of: peace.

They might even say they are 'comfortable' with the abusive relationship. But comfortable is a label that only applies to that which provides physical comfort, encourages peace, well-being, or physical ease. It means to be happy or relaxed, enjoying or providing a position of contentment and security. No one can truly be 'comfortable' with being abused or hit all the time.

When a victim who has left an abusive situation realizes what they are feeling is not a lack of comfort, but a feeling they are unfamiliar with, they have taken another step toward healing.

The only way to get familiar with a new situation is to live through it, enduring the unfamiliar feeling for a while and getting comfortable with the fact that you will be in unfamiliar situations as you are healing. Even when you are in a safe community, starting to recognize peace and safety, you may find that healing can be awkward, messy, and uncomfortable—and tremendously good.

## In Summary

There are many reasons people may stay in abusive relationships. Even when a person recognizes they are in an abusive relationship, they may stay in that situation because to change feels dangerous too. However, they will need to move through the unfamiliar in order to get out of abuse.

# CHAPTER 16

## What Does It Take to Get Out?

Sometimes an abuse victim can finally make a choice to leave an abuser without help from others. But many times, they need help to be able to leave. Adult victims need a plan and resources: where to go, how to have food, shelter, clothing, and safety after leaving. Child victims need an adult to listen to them and look at their situation and make a report to the authorities so they can get help.

### Resources Needed

What is the plan? What are the resources needed to leave? It is helpful to have money and to know phone numbers of places to call, who can you call, where can you go. What kind of things do you need to take with you? A parent with children who is leaving an abusive situation may need the children's birth certificates and any custody papers. It is also good to have some basic clothes for all of you to wear. Look up resources about which shelters have space. What are different places you could go to that help people who are in an abusive situation to escape it? Do you have family or friends you could reconnect with once you are in a safe place?

But getting to a safe place is just the first step in healing. Next is learning how to start life again Working in therapy with a counselor is an important part of healing and growth for anyone leaving an abusive situation. Being able to connect with a safe someone that you can tell your story to, someone who is objective and supportive and will help you look at the emotional wounds that are lingering, is an effective part of the way to move past the abuse. The barriers that make it hard for you to connect with people and reconnect with safe family and friends need to be addressed. Working with a mental health counselor can give you the strength and emotional support you need as you work though these barriers.

Sometimes it means making new friends and creating for yourself a new connected family. If you grew up in an abusive situation, you may choose an abusive partner because the attitudes seemed familiar. But you can be the generation that changes a legacy of abuse in your family. You could make a change so that your children do not repeat that pattern. You can be that generation that breaks the generational curse and opens up your family to a healthier life.

### Reporting Suspected Child Abuse

In the United States, there are laws against abuse and the laws require some people to be mandatory reporters of suspected abuse. We want victims to get the help they need to be safe. Mandatory reporters work in jobs that come in contact with vulnerable populations, like medical professionals, educational professionals, and others. However, all of us can help. Any person can make a report if they suspect a vulnerable person or child is being abused. Anyone can call the police or a child abuse hotline.

## What Happens When Child Abuse Is Reported.

If you think someone is being hurt or is in danger, call 911 immediately. You can report child abuse to the child abuse hotline or by calling local law enforcement. Generally, who makes the report of abuse is kept anonymous. As the old saying points out, "It takes a village to raise a child." I think all of us have a moral duty to report when a child or vulnerable adult is being hurt.

The response to the report of suspected child abuse will vary. Child Protective Services will take down information and if they feel they have enough information and merit, they will investigate. They are going to look at the safety of that child. Sometimes what they do is assess if this family needs extra support; if so, they will provide the resources the family needs in order to make the children's lives better. They may require that the family gets parenting training and counseling, so the family learns better ways to cope with stress and better ways to discipline children.

Sometimes Child Protective Services finds they have to remove the children from the situation because it's too unsafe: the children are in too much risk of harm. In this case, the children are taken out of the home and put in a temporary foster home. They may provide, encourage, or require that for the parents to get their children back, the parents need to go through counseling and classes and training so they can learn to create a safe home environment for the children. When the home is assessed to be safe, the children are returned.

Sometimes when Child Protective Services put the children in foster care until the parents can provide a safe home, the parents refuse to accept services and learn how to make the home safer. After a reasonable period of trying to work with uncooperative parents, the parents' rights are terminated, and that temporary foster home placement may become a permanent adoption.

## What Happens in the Family When Abuse Is Reported?

Child abuse creates a world of pain for all who are touched by it. It is important to remember that the source of the pain is not the *reporting* of the abuse. The source of all the disruption is the violation that happened when someone chose to abuse a child. It is not the child's fault all this pain happened in the family. However, when abuse is reported, the family and the extended family are going to have pain. If the abuser was living in the home, that person may have to leave the home for a time. For example: the abuser and the victim may not be allowed to live in the same home until some healing takes place. When a child is sexually abused by dad, either dead or the child may have to leave the home for a while. It is a painful place for a child to be. The family may blame the abused child for the breakup of the family instead of facing the fact that it is the abuser's fault for abusing, not the child's fault for reporting it. When someone chooses to abuse a child, everyone gets hurt.

## Outcomes of Not Reporting

When child abuse is not reported, the child has no advocate to help them get out of a situation they are powerless to escape on their own. Some of the outcomes of not reporting child abuse are that the child grows up with no resources. They may not understand that they were abused. Sometimes the abuse is so bad the child dies because no one reported the abuse to take the child out of that unsafe situation. Sometimes the child grows up crippled by that trauma and their adult life is hindered until they can go through a healing process.

## What keeps people from reporting abuse

- Some people don't want to interfere with other people's business.
    o *But is it everybody's business that children and vulnerable adults have the opportunity to live in a safe environment.*
- People would know who reported and be mad at me.
    o *Most reports can be reported anonymously.*

There is a possibility someone would be upset about your report, we measure that against what about the risk to the child. Would we rather have another adult upset with us or would live with the fact that a child died because no one stepped in to help them?

## Call national reporting hotline

Reporting Suspected Child Abuse or Neglect by Telephone. Call 1-800-4ACHILD (1-800-422-4453). All reports can be kept anonymous, although you may be encouraged to give your name. This hotline has access to a network of welfare agencies around the country and can direct your report to the proper authorities.

## In Summary

It can be hard to escape an abusive situation. When leaving an abusive situation, a person should make sure they know where to go for the resources they will need. There are online resources to help people get connected. We want victims to get the help they need to be safe. In the United States, there are laws against abuse and the laws require some people to be mandatory reporters of suspected abuse. Anyone can make a report if they suspect a vulnerable person or child is being abused.

# CHAPTER 17

---

## Healing After Disruption

Restoration and healing are possible! I'm a strong believer that restoration is possible, that individuals and families can be healed of the trauma of abuse. People can truly escape—from beyond victim, beyond survivor—to be a healthy human. Redemption is even possible for those who have abused others. But that redemption takes a lot of work for people who have abused to come to the point where they want to choose to be redeemed and make changes. You cannot make somebody else change. If people choose not to change, then all you can do is adapt to the behavior. If a person chooses to continue in abusive behaviors, your choice is to put up with being abused and being a victim, or to leave, or to set boundaries and keep them. You can choose not to be treated in that way any longer. It will not help someone who abuses to find redemption if they can continue to abuse. That pattern of abuse will continue in a downward spiral until and unless the abuser decides to change.

## Repairing Damage in Family Network

I have found the healing of the family network after abuse needs to begin in the individuals who choose to face the truth and heal and grow. It may start with one individual who chooses the healing path. Later, as the beneficial growth becomes evident, others may also choose healing.

Working with a professional mental health counselor is vital during the healing and growth stage. The trauma of abuse creates deep wounds that a therapist can help you clean out so they can heal. It is a complex process that will take some time, so having a mental health professional help guide you is very helpful.

## What to Tell the Children

When you are telling your children about the disruption that happened in the family, why some people are not seen any more, always speak truth. Abuse and evil thrive in silence and lies. But all the details of the truth may not be appropriate to share with young children. Speak age-appropriate truth and discretionary truth, but always truth. It is not appropriate to discuss details of violence , assault, sexual abuse with young children. But you can still say truth – age appropriate truth.

When your child grows to be an adult and they look back at what you told them about this time, when the family had stress and trouble they will see you spoke truth, or will they see that you lied to them. You do not have to tell them all the details, it may not be appropriate. For example the way to speak of it may be to say that *'Grandpa needed to learn how to treat children better, how not to hurt children and therefore we had to be away from grandpa until he could learn that."* When your child is an adult, and they look back and understand more of what that was about but also that you told them truth and they can trust you.

You have to decide who needs to know what. There is a difference between "want" to know, "need" to know and "right" to know. What do we want to know? Likely everything about everything. But what do we need to know? Just the things we have to make decisions about. We need to know information about risk, so we can keep our children and ourselves safe. What do we have a right to know? Things that affect our lives. Gossip is generally about "want" to know. Gossiping damages trust and can break connections. When you hear a bit of information, before you say it to others, ask yourself: is this public information I could share with others right in front of the person it is about without causing them discomfort or shame? Will it build them up? Is this private information I have no right to pass on to someone else? What is my purpose in passing on this information? Is it to strengthen and encourage? Is it to tear down? Do I even know if this is true? If I need to share the info, can I share it in a way that is respectful, objective, and helpful?

**Forgiveness and Safety**

Forgiveness is a part of the healing process. It is a vital piece to restoring and strengthening healthy connections. Forgiveness is a choice of will, not just a feeling. The choice to forgive may be today's decision, but it may take a lot of tomorrows for the forgiveness process to be worked through. We can make a choice to forgive while our feelings are still intense, we still hurt, and have some anger. The choice to forgive does not rely on feelings.

Just because we forgive does not mean we need to put ourselves at risk again with someone who has broken our trust. I can treat them respectfully, and still not trust them. The amount of respect I choose to give others is more about me than it is about them. I do not have to agree with their choices. I do not have to accept their behavior towards me. I can respectfully say no to them.

We may have lingering anger over the treatment of the past. We can use those angry feelings to make real change. When we use self-control to harness our own anger in respectful and healthy ways, we can thoughtfully make decisions that have a good chance of moving towards real change. When we use our anger to fuel bad choices and disrespectful behavior, we are choosing to destroy and tear down.

There can be people who have treated us badly who we still love. Often, these people are in our immediate and extended family. We need to love them enough to get them the help they need to make changes. Some people choose to be evil, and they cannot be helped while they are active in that choice. Other people can be helped. They want to connect, and they may be willing to make a change in their life. Maybe they do not know how we can say no and yet still love them. But we can love them enough to not put up with bad behavior and being abused. Putting up with abuse is detrimental to both people.

There is a risk involved in confronting an abuse or leaving an abuser. There is also risk involved in not confronting and not leaving. Perhaps there is less risk in leaving than there is in staying.

## Help for Abusers

Many, but not all, abusers can be helped. But rarely are they ever helped by somebody continuing to put up with the abuse. That just sends them on a downward spiral into deeper abuse.

It may be necessary to separate from an abuser so both parties can get help individually. The victim can get help learning how to be healthy, how to set good boundaries, and how to interact in ways that are helpful for themselves and their children. An abuser may need to learn how to be alone—how to be good company to themselves—before they can learn how to interact with others. It may take months for people to heal enough to then be able to decide if they want to work toward rebuilding their relationship. They both need to learn how to have better interactions, better connections. An important part of healing is learning how to set boundaries, defining what is yours and what is not yours and learning how to respect boundaries and not push again people's boundaries. It is also about learning how to sit with discomfort when life is not what I like, not seeking to have someone fix it for you, but to strengthen your abilities simply to be there in an uncomfortable space for a time, and mature in your responses to stress.

Another part of it is learning how to communicate. How do I in a healthy way learn how to ask for what I need? How do I speak to authority? How do I listen to people when they're telling me what they need? How do we work together to find solutions where both people get what they need? How do I take no for an answer and not push against the no? How do I adapt to what the answer is? How do I fight fair?

Fighting fair is an important skill for people who are connected to other people because all of us have disagreements. It's a normal part of our connectedness to have disagreements. Being able to express my needs and my wants, and listen to your needs and your wants, and then figure out where we disagree and how to adapt is a complicated but necessary process for healthy connections. Some things we can compromise on. Some things we have to agree to disagree and how do we treat people respectfully when we're in the midst of that. And then beyond that how do we nurture each other build another up.

*Therefore encourage one another and build each other up, just as in fact you are doing.*

*1 Thessalonians 5:11*

## In Summary

Healing is possible after abuse and disruption. Connections can be healed, if each party wants to the hard work of healing. There is a joy-filled life available past the trauma of abuse, bullying, and chaos. There is an abundant life waiting for you!

# CHAPTER 18

## Life After Healing

Your life after healing is ready for abundance. You have grown in your skills of being connected in healthy ways. You are now more able to be a safe person and recognize other safe people.

### You Have Come a Long Way

Throughout this book, we explored many of the ways we are connected to ourselves and to others. We contrasted healthy ways to connect with good boundaries with unhealthy ways connections can be manipulative, unsafe, or abusive.

You have explored the ways that our values strengthen or weaken our connections. We looked at some step-by-step ways you can increase your skills in the art of good relationships.

Finally, we explored how connections can be disrupted by be manipulation, aggression, and abuse. We discussed what can lead some people toward abusive behavior and why it is hard for victims to leave unhealthy relationships.

You have the principles of growth and healing in this book, and throughout this entire Trauma Healing Series. If you put into practice all of the principles you have learned here, you may change your life in major ways for the better. Even if you make only some changes, your life can be calmer, more fulfilling, and less lonely. Change is difficult. But healing is possible. Don't stop here.

## Don't Get Stuck

The journey to healing can be long and have many segments. Let me encourage you to take the whole journey. Don't get stuck along the way.

- **Victimized.** Bad things really do happen to people. There are times when people are the victim of the negative actions of others. Sometimes we recognize this long after we experienced the trauma.

  o **Healthy Response.** Recognizing that you were victimized is an important step on the path to healing. Take time to see the truth. Take time to grieve the loss and betrayal. Take time to acknowledge and process painful emotions.

  o **Getting Stuck.** Accepting a victim mentality that bad things will always happen; other people are always to blame for my misery;

any effort on my part to change will fail, so there is no use in trying. Getting stuck here is to wallow in negativity and blame it on others, avoiding responsibility, making excuses, and not seeking solutions.

o **Moving Forward.** Make some small action that can lead to improvement. Look for what you are responsible for and be accountable to make progress. Begin working toward healing and change.

- **Outraged.** When we recognize that we were victimized, we can move from helpless victim to feeling a sense of righteous indignation, anger, rage, or resentment.

  o **Healthy Response.** It is not wrong to feel anger. Anger is the normal and natural response to experiencing victimization. A healthy response is to find safe, respectful ways to acknowledge and work through the anger to bring positive change.

  o **Getting Stuck.** We could feel like the whole world is against us. We feel anger at everyone and everything. We doubt anyone cares about the injustice, pain, and misery we have experienced. We doubt justice exists. We can feel angry and resentful of people who seem happy and successful. We can isolate and feel depressed and alone, and behave badly.

  o **Moving Forward.** Find a safe place to express what you are feeling. Working with a mental health professional can be helpful to explore healthy ways to process these feelings and move forward. Use the intensity to make positive changes in your life and in the world.

- **Survived.** When we recognize that we were victimized, we acknowledge the anger, and now we have survived. That is a significant milestone on the journey of healing.

  o **Healthy Response.** Recognize and celebrate this milestone. Take the time to look back and see how far you have come. Affirm your growth and the skills you have gained.

  o **Getting Stuck.** We define all of our life as someone who has survived trauma. The things we do are measured as done by a survivor. The accomplishments of our day-to-day growth are identified as done by a survivor.

  o **Moving Forward.** Look toward to your future as what you can do now, as you are now. Assess your skills, interests, abilities, and gifts as they are now and move confidently into the future.

## Move On to an Abundant Life

When we were hurt by abuse and trauma, we were a victim. As we begin to heal, we can be outraged that we were violated. As we work through a healing process, we became a survivor. But all those stages are defined by the original trauma. It is time to move forward into an abundant life that is no longer defined by the traumas of the past. Find confidence, contentment, and happiness in a healthy life no longer hindered by the troubles of the past. This is the theme of book four in this Trauma Healing Series, *Abundance*.

## A Week in a Healthy, Connected Life

Joe and Mary start each day with some loving words, friendly conversation, and planning what their family would be doing for the day. With a hug and a kiss, the family goes on their ways with the knowledge they are loved and cared for.

At work, Joe has a good reputation for being reliable and a diligent worker. He is well-liked and friendly with his co-workers. Mary's coworkers appreciate her positive attitude and generous spirit. Both Joe and Mary enjoy their time at work and have a good work/life balance.

When the family comes together in the evenings, they are interested in listening to each other about how the day went. They share a meal and spend some time doing the home chores. Then they have time for individual and sometimes joint hobbies and entertainment activities.

When the weekend comes, they connect with extended family and with friends. Joe and Mary build into their life ways to get done what needs doing and yet still have time to connect with the people they care about. They make time to connect with their spiritual family as well, those who share their core spiritual belief.

## In Summary

Not everyone's life goes easy all the time. But when we make it our intention to connect in healthy ways with people, we can begin to blend more and more healthy moments of connection into our life, bringing us more joy and happiness and moving us toward a more abundant life!

# Afterword

---

## Faith's Story of Connections

As a young and abused child, I had figured out the minimum amount of connection required to survive. Decades of my life were spent living with trauma. I grew up in a Christian and abusive home. Christian and abusive are two words that should not be together, but they were in my childhood experience. I grew up in the midst of extreme poverty, occasional homelessness, and all kinds of abuse. I yearned for connection with others, but always found it painful within my family and I was forbidden to connect with others outside the family. I had that rule beaten into me.

My deepest connections were with God, myself, nature, and books during all those years. I am by nature an introvert who enjoys time alone. However, I need connection with people too. We all do. This book series shows you the important relationship skills of how to connect deeply with yourself and from that solid core how to connect in healthy ways with others.

My understanding of how the world works is that God cherishes being loved and He gave us free will so that we could choose to love Him or choose not to. That ability to choose or choose not to is a precious thing. When we freely choose to love God, it is glorious. But God will not make us love Him; He invites us to love Him. He gave us free will. We get to choose how we will live and what we will value. People therefore sometimes use their free will to hurt themselves and hurt others. I was hurt a lot as a child by the choices of others. When I say that I am safe in God's care, I know that eternally I am safe. When I die, I will go to be with Him in heaven, in that glorious presence. Everything my heart desires is there: my heart desires Him.

When God took me through a healing process, it included healing my ability to make connections with others. Over a three-and-a-half-year period, I learned how to make friends, how to find people who can be trusted, how to connect deeply with people, and what it means to have many levels of friends. I went from having four people in my life (who all shared my last name) to having over 60 friends came to celebrate my graduation with a master's degree in counseling. I learned about the way healthy boundaries allow me to connect safely. I know what it means to go from isolated to having a wealth of good connections.

Growing up in that Christian and abusive home, I experienced many kinds of abuse, extreme poverty, chaos, and having no settled home. As an adult, I spent many years affected by the lingering effects of that trauma. It affected all the choices that I made, it affected the way that I lived, it affected the way that I raised my child. The trauma we experience in childhood affects our daily life in the present. Sure, that trauma was in the past, but the effects are being lived out in the present. The unhealthy patterns of life will not go away on their own.

For instance, when trust is violated, the ability to trust again may be hard. That reluctance to trust can show up in a relationship with a significant other. It may be difficult to trust a landlord. It may be hard to trust a boss. Making friends can be hard. When we have a difficulty trusting, it may be hard for us to make good healthy connections with any people, it is hard to even know what a good connection would look like.

After growing up with a lack of safety, I really wanted to be safe as an adult. The trouble was the only way I knew how to be safe was to be alone. I did not feel comfortable alone, and yet it was the only way I could figure out to keep from being hurt by people. I did not know how to let people get to know me without risk. I figured out a way to work self-employed, alone at home, rarely having to interact with people.

I had gotten used to being comfortable with a lot of uncomfortable things. I was dealing with post-traumatic stress and would have a high level of anxiety when I would need to get groceries. I figured out how to shop once a month so that I could lower how often I had to go into stores. Every time I was in a store, my anxiety was so intense. When I would go to check out, I would feel almost a panic attack with somebody standing too close behind me. And yet I did not see that as a problem; I just saw it as the way life was.

When I would go out to have fun, I would put my child in the car and we would drive to the beach, and then we would find a spot that wasn't very populated on the beach and then we would walk and splash in the waves alone and then we walk back to our car and drive back alone a couple hours back to our home alone. We would have a lot of fun doing that, but it's even more fun to spend time with people. I didn't know how to be safe with people yet. I didn't know how to not let people take advantage of my vulnerability.

When God got my attention and nudged me toward healing, I finally decided to go through a healing process for this trauma. I started reluctantly, not wanting to, but I knew it was time. I needed to heal this pain out of my life. My healing journey included a supportive group, individual counseling with a mental health therapist, reading lots of self-help books, classes on helpful topics, and attending a home fellowship group through my church.

I was careful and cautious; healing often felt awkward, messy, and uncomfortable, but the result was very good. There was a synergy in how God worked through all of these things to bring healing to my life. The panic was gone, the PTSD was healed, and my life was turned in a new direction.

My healing journey included:

- Support group for adult women who have been abused as a child. I went every week and sat there quietly, with my PTSD triggering, feeling levels of panic and fear trying to sit into the room and feel safe. But I kept going back every week because somewhere here was the healing I was looking for. I was not alone in dealing with these kinds of issues and it turned out there were other people dealing with the same things.
- Individual counseling sessions every week. Even there I felt panic every time I went into that session. But I continued to go because there was healing there, I could feel it, I knew it.
- Classes learning more about the Bible and about God. Because of the spiritual abuse I suffered in a Christian and abusive home, I was trying to figure out what was true and what was not true in regard to my faith. There was healing in the classes.
- Books on abuse recovery, anxiety, depression, and stress. I read a lot of books trying to understand why I had this panic, why was it so deep, why was it so strongly held. There was healing in the books.
- Home fellowship group, Bible study group. Here I learned how to be connected to Christian people in healthy ways. There was healing in that supportive group.

Through many different resources I was prayerfully trying to find the pieces that applied to me, the pieces that would help me escape the pain and darkness.

My experience shows me that when life is in chaos, God is here with me, comforting my heart. Being safe in God's care does not mean he is going to protect me from the things that are going on in the world. It means he protects my heart and my mind. He gives me a way out, a way to be resilient

A lot of my life has been uncertain and difficult, but I have seen God's love and care in the hard places. When I would call out to him, he would comfort my heart and my mind. I read his Word and its words of comfort for other people who have struggled. When I am connected to God's people in church groups and home Bible study groups, these people would care about me. We are made to be connected to others in the body of Christ. It is kind of God's love with flesh on.

God loves me even when life is not what I like. God is more concerned with my character development than my comfort. I have a tendency to be more concerned with my comfort. I like to be comfortable, but it is during the uncomfortable times that my character can develop. In those times, I get to choose if am I going to stay true to God and my integrity. Am I going to do what is right and proper even when things are hard? I get to choose whether I am going to love and trust God when life is hard.

Jesus is the way. In John 3:16 it stated that "God so loved the world that he sent his only son that whosoever believes in him should not perish but have eternal life." I find that such a wonderfully comforting statement. The "whosoever" means this offer is open to me. It's open to anybody and everybody. No one is too bad or too wrong or too different. God made all of us. The offer is something we have to accept in order to have the eternal life he offers. When we accept Jesus as Savior and Lord, we are agreeing with God that we have done wrong. Confessing to him what we have done and accepting him into our life as Lord and Savior gives us salvation. The Lord part means that then I want to obey him. He is not going to make me obey him, but because I love him and because he loves me, I want to obey. So, I spend time reading his Word. I spend time with his people, so I am connected and growing more like him.

This invitation to abundant life is open to anyone and everyone. Not everyone chooses to accept Jesus as Lord and Savior, but that is who he is in my life. He is my savior, my lord, my friend, and my guide to a healthy life.

The fundamental principles I taught you in this book will help you tremendously to have a healthier life. They will help you to understand your rights and your value as you go through the trials of life. But the really deep calm, that solid, unshakable peace welling from the depth of inside of you, that comes from knowing, loving, and following Jesus.

# Other books by Faith Winters

Made in the USA
Monee, IL
20 August 2021

75436700R00089